C. Hubert H. (Charles Hubert Hastings) Perry

Six lyrics from Elizabethan song-books

set as part-songs

C. Hubert H. (Charles Hubert Hastings) Perry

Six lyrics from Elizabethan song-books
set as part-songs

ISBN/EAN: 9783741174353

Manufactured in Europe, USA, Canada, Australia, Japa

Cover: Foto ©Thomas Meinert / pixelio.de

Manufactured and distributed by brebook publishing software
(www.brebook.com)

C. Hubert H. (Charles Hubert Hastings) Perry

Six lyrics from Elizabethan song-books

LYRICS

FROM THE SONG-BOOKS OF THE
ELIZABETHAN AGE.

LYRICS FROM THE SONG-BOOKS OF THE ELIZABETHAN AGE.

EDITED BY

A. H. BULLEN.

LONDON :—LAWRENCE AND BULLEN, Ltd.
16, HENRIETTA ST., COVENT GARDEN. 1897.

From Automated Records Support Services Unit,
220 N Library.

To _____ Stacks _____ Library

Call no.

821.08
B871y   Entry: _____ Bullen

               Title: _____ Lyrics from Elizabethan song books

The indicated change is being made for this title.
Please have your book remarked. The existing records
in LCS and FBR will be corrected.

Call no. change: _____ 821.08 B871Y

Holdings change: _____

                        Thank you,
                        Lois Smestad

NOTE.

About eighteen months ago I published a collection of Lyrics from the Song-books of the Elizabethan Age; *and this was followed recently by a second collection,* More Lyrics from the Song-books of the Elizabethan Age.

The present book consists of poems selected from those two volumes. In the preface to More Lyrics *I announced that I intended to publish such an anthology as is here offered to the reader.*

August, 1888.

In the third edition a few textual corrections have been introduced, and the editor has succeeded in discovering the authorship of some songs that he had previously failed to identify.

July, 1891.

Some additional corrections have been introduced in the fourth edition.

October, 1896.

PREFACE.

IN Elizabethan times the art of song-writing was carried to perfection. Composers were not then content to regard the words of a song as a mere peg on which to hang the music, but sought the services of true-born lyrists. The old song-books preserve many graceful and delightful poems that would otherwise have perished. Some of these collections are extant only in unique exemplars preserved in the library of the British Museum, the Bodleian, the library of the Royal College of Music, or in private libraries : for others I have had to go to MSS. in the British Museum or at Oxford. The object that I have kept in view is to make my anthology at once novel and interesting. Well-known poems, or poems that ought to be well known, I have avoided ; and, on the other hand, no poem has been included merely on account of its rarity.

A book may be very rare and very worthless : that I admit. But an examination of the present volume will show that some choice lyrics have lain hidden out of sight for nearly three centuries. How many readers have heard of Captain Tobias Hume? He published in 1605 "The First Part of Airs, French, Polish and others together." Among these Airs I found the flawless verses that I have placed at the beginning of my anthology, "Fain would I change that note." Surely few, even among the very elect, have sung Love's praises in happier accents of heartfull devotion. Captain Hume wrote the music, but I know not who wrote the verses. It may be assumed that the composers, as a rule, were only responsible for the music. Dr. Thomas Campion, of whom I shall speak presently, was both a poet and a musician; but he was an exception to the rule.

Take another example, the sweet and tender lullaby,[1] worthy of William Blake, "Upon my lap my sovereign sits." It is from Martin Peerson's "Private Music," 1620, of which only one perfect copy, preserved in the Bodleian Library, is extant.

---

[1] I must now add (October, 1896) that I was wrong in supposing that this lullaby is found only in Peerson's Song-book. It forms part of a poem (of twenty-four stanzas) by the Roman Catholic poet Robert Verstegan, which was printed in his rare book of *Odes*, 1601. The complete poem, which is far too long, has been recently reprinted in Mr. Orby Shipley's "Carmina Mariana," an anthology in praise of Our Lady. Peerson selected the best stanzas.

From the same song-book I have taken the graceful and playful dialogue—"Open the door! Who's there within?"—between an eager wooer and a discreet maid; and other dainty little songs.

A large and important collection of early MS. music-books is preserved in the library of Christ Church, Oxford. Here I found the fine verses beginning, "Yet if his Majesty our sovereign lord." The detailed description of the preparations made by a loyal subject for the entertainment of his "earthly king" is singularly impressive. Few could have dealt with common household objects —tables and chairs and candles and the rest—in so dignified a spirit. Our poet has triumphed over the difficulties :—

> "'Set me fine Spanish tables in the hall,
> See they be fitted all ;
> Let there be room to eat,
> And order taken that there want no meat.
> See every sconce and candlestick made bright,
> That without tapers they may give a light.
> Look to the presence : are the carpets spread,
> The dais o'er the head,
> The cushions in the chairs,
> And all the candles lighted on the stairs?
> Perfume the chamber, and in any case
> Let each man give attendance in his place.'"

It would be hard to improve on that description. Then the contrast between these preparations made

for an earthly king and the reception provided for
the King of Heaven !—

> "But at the coming of the King of Heaven
> All's set at six and seven ;
> We wallow in our sin,
> Christ cannot find a chamber in the inn.
> We entertain him always like a stranger,
> And as at first still lodge him in the manger."

The volume which contains this fine poem has
more than one lyric, set to music, of Henry Vaughan
the Silurist. Am I right in surmising that this
unpublished poem is also by Vaughan? I know
no other devotional poet who could have written
it. Whether it be Vaughan's or not, I am glad to
include it in my anthology. I trust that the other
Christ Church songs will also be acceptable. The
odd little snatch, " Hey nonny no! Men are fools
that wish to die!" almost takes one's breath away
by the vehemence of its rapture. "Daphnis came
on a summer's day" is as good as the best things
in Bateson's madrigals (no slight praise), and "Art
thou that she than whom no fairer is?" might have
come from one of Robert Jones' song-books. The
frog's wooing of the crab, "There was a frog swum
in the lake," is a capital piece of fooling, almost
worthy to rank with Ravenscroft's "It was the frog
in the well." It was set to music by Alfonso

Ferrabosco, but is not found in that composer's printed " Airs."

The earliest of the Elizabethan song-writers was William Byrd. In the year of the Spanish Armada, 1588, he published "Psalms, Sonnets, and Songs of Sadness and Piety," the first Elizabethan song-book of importance. He was probably a native of Lincoln, and was born in, or about, 1538.[1] From 1563 to 1569 he was organist of Lincoln Cathedral, and on 22 February, 1569-70, he was appointed Gentleman of the Chapel Royal. In 1598 he became possessed of Stondon Place, Essex. He adhered to the Roman Catholic faith; and his wife, Ellen Birley (by whom he had five children), was also a zealous Romanist. His last work was published in 1611, and he died at a ripe old age on 24 July, 1623. The "Psalms, Sonnets, and Songs" are dedicated to Sir Christopher Hatton. From the title one would gather that the collection was mainly of a sacred character, but in

[1] I have made no attempt to give any full biographical account of the composers. Excellent notices of Byrd and John Dowland, by Mr. Barclay Squire, may be seen in the "Dictionary of National Biography." A full account of Dr. Thomas Campion is prefixed to my edition of Campion's Works (privately printed). For notices of the other composers I must be content to refer the reader to Grove's "Dictionary of Music."

an epistle to the reader Byrd hastens to set us right
on that point: "Benign reader, here is offered
unto thy courteous acceptance music of sundry
sorts, and to content divers humours. If thou be
disposed to pray, here are psalms; if to be merry
here are sonnets." There is, indeed, fare for all
comers; and a reader has only himself to blame
if he goes away dissatisfied. In those days, as in
these, it was not uncommon for a writer to attribute
all faults, whether of omission or commission, to the
luckless printer. Byrd, on the other hand, solemnly
warns us that "in the expression of these songs
either by voices or instruments, if there be any jar
or dissonance," we are not to blame the printer, who
has been at the greatest pains to secure accuracy.
Then the composer makes a modest appeal on behalf of himself, requesting those who find any fault
in the composition "either with courtesy to let the
same be concealed," or "in friendly sort" point out
the errors, which shall be corrected in a future
impression. This is the proper manner of dealing
between gentlemen. His next publication was
"Songs of Sundry Natures," 1589, which was
dedicated to Sir Henry Carey, first Lord Hunsdon,
who seems to have been as staunch a patron of
Byrd as his son, Sir George Carey, was of Dowland.
In 1611 appeared Byrd's last work, " Psalms, Songs,

and Sonnets." The composer must have taken to
heart the precepts set down by Sir Edward Dyer in
" My mind to me a kingdom is " (printed in "Psalms,
Sonnets, and Songs "), for his dedicatory epistle and
his address to the reader show him to have been a
man who had laid up a copious store of genial wisdom,
upon which he could draw freely in the closing days
of an honourable life. His earlier works had been
well received, and in addressing "all true lovers of
music" he knew that he could rely upon their
cordial sympathy. "I am much encouraged," he
writes, "to commend to you these my last labours,
for mine *ultimum vale*"; and then follows a piece
of friendly counsel: "Only this I desire, that you
will be as careful to hear them well expressed, as I
have been both in the composing and correcting of
them. Otherwise the best song that ever was made
will seem harsh and unpleasant; for that the well
expressing of them either by voices or instruments
is the life of our labours, which is seldom or never
well performed at the first singing or playing."
Quaint old-fashioned moral verses were much
affected by Byrd, particularly in his latest song-
book. He inculcates precepts of homely piety in
a cheerful spirit, with occasional touches of naïve
epigrammatic terseness. Many men strongly object to be bullied from a pulpit, but he must be a

born churl who could be offended at such an
exhortation as the following :—

> " Let not the sluggish sleep
> Close up thy waking eye,
> Until with judgement deep
> Thy daily deeds thou try :
> He that one sin in conscience keeps
> When he to quiet goes,
> More vent'rous is than he that sleeps
> With twenty mortal foes."

No musician of the Elizabethan age was more
famous than John Dowland, whose "heavenly
touch upon the lute" was commended in a well-
known sonnet (long attributed to Shakespeare) by
Richard Barnfield. Dowland was born at West-
minster in 1562. At the age of twenty, or there-
abouts, he started on his travels; and, after
rambling through "the chiefest parts of France, a
nation furnished with great variety of music," he
bent his course "towards the famous province of
Germany," where he found "both excellent masters
and most honourable patrons of music." In the
course of his travels he visited Venice, Padua, Genoa,
Ferrara and Florence, gaining applause everywhere
by his musical skill. On his return to England he
took his degree at Oxford as Bachelor of Music in
1588. In 1597 he published " The First Book of
Songs or Airs of four parts, with Tableture for the

Lute." Prefixed is a dedicatory epistle to Sir George Carey, second Lord Hunsdon, in which the composer alludes gracefully to the kindness that he had received from Lady Elizabeth Carey, the patroness of Spenser. A "Second Book of Songs or Airs" was published in 1600, when the composer was at the Danish Court, serving as lutenist to Christian IV. The work was dedicated to the famous Lucy Countess of Bedford, whom Ben Jonson immortalized in a noble sonnet. From a curious address to the reader by George Eastland, the publisher, it would appear that in spite of Dowland's high reputation the sale of his works was not very profitable. "If the consideration of mine own estate," writes Eastland, "or the true worth of money, had prevailed with me above the desire of pleasing you and showing my love to my friends, these second labours of Master Dowland—whose very name is a large preface of commendation to the book—had for ever lain in darkness, or at the least frozen in a cold and foreign country." The expenses of publication were heavy, but he consoled himself with the thought that his high-spirited enterprise would be appreciated by a select audience. In 1603 appeared "The Third and Last Book of Songs or Airs;" and in 1612, when he was lutenist to Lord Walden, Dowland issued

his last work, " A Pilgrim's Solace." He is supposed
to have died about 1615, leaving a son, Robert
Dowland, who gained credit as a composer.
Some modern critics have judged that Dowland's
music was overrated by his contemporaries, and
that he is wanting in variety and originality.
Whether these critics are right or wrong, it would
be difficult to overrate the poetry. In attempting
to select representative lyrics one is embarrassed
by the wealth of material. The rich clusters of
golden verse hang so temptingly that it is hard to
cease plucking when once we have begun.

Byrd and Dowland are distinguished names in
the annals of Elizabethan song, but unquestion-
ably Dr. Thomas Campion is greater than either.
Campion wrote not only the music, but the poetry
for his songs—he was at once an eminent composer
and a lyric poet of the first rank. He published
a volume of Latin verse which displays fluency and
elegance and wit ; as a masque-writer he was hardly
inferior to Ben Jonson : and he was the author of
treatises on music and poetry. We first hear of him
in 1586, when he was admitted a member of Gray's
Inn (Harl. MS. 1912, "Admittances to Gray's
Inn "). Conceiving a distaste for legal studies, he
applied himself to medicine and practised with
success as a physician. His earliest work was

"Epigrammatum Libri Duo," originally published
in 1595,[1] and republished with additions in 1619,
the year of his death. Francis Meres, in "Wit's
Treasury," 1598, mentions Campion among the
"English men, being Latin poets," who had
"attained good report and honourable advance-
ment in the Latin tongue." But many of the
English lyrics must have been written,[2] though they
were not collected, towards the close of the sixteenth century. So early as 1593, George Peele
made a complimentary reference to Campion in
the prologue to the "Honour of the Garter."
W[illiam] C[lerke] in "Polimanteia," 1595, speaks
of "sweet Master Campion," obviously in reference
to his English poems ; and in Harleian MS. 6910,
which was written circ. 1596, there are three English poems by Campion. We may therefore assume
that many of his best songs were written in the last
decade of the sixteenth century. In 1601 Campion
and Philip Rosseter published jointly " A Book of

---

[1] Only one perfect copy of the 1595 edition is known. It
was recently discovered by Mr. W. II. Allnutt (of the
Bodleian) in the library of Lord Robartes. An imperfect
copy is in the Bodleian.

[2] "Hark, all you ladies" (p. 169) is one of the poems
("of sundrie other Noblemen and Gentlemen ") annexed to
the surreptitious edition (Newman's) of Sidney's *Astrophel
and Stella*, 1591.

Airs." The music was partly written by Campion
and partly by Rosseter; but the whole of the .
poetry belongs to Campion. From the dedicatory
epistle, by Rosseter, to Sir Thomas Monson, we
learn that Campion's songs, "made at his vacant
hours and privately imparted to his friends," had
been passed from hand to hand, and had suffered
from the carelessness of successive transcribers.
Some impudent persons, we are told, had "unre-
spectively challenged" (*i.e.* claimed) the credit
both of the music and the poetry. The address to
the reader, which follows the dedicatory epistle,
is unsigned, but appears to have been written by
Campion. "What epigrams are in poetry," it
begins, "the same are airs in music : then in their
chief perfection when they are short and well
seasoned. But to clog a light song with a long
preludium is to corrupt the nature of it. Many
rests in music were invented either for necessity of
the fugue or granted as an harmonical licence in
songs of many parts; but in airs I find no use they
have, unless it be to make a vulgar and trivial
modulation seem to the ignorant strange and to
the judicial tedious." It is odd that this true poet,
who had so exquisite a sense of form, and whose
lyrics are frequently triumphs of metrical. skill,
should have published a treatise ("Observations in

the Art of English Poesy ") to prove that the use
of rhyme should be discontinued and that English
metres should be fashioned after classical models.
"Poesy," he writes, "in all kind of speaking is
the chief beginner and maintainer of eloquence,
not only helping the ear with the acquaintance of
sweet numbers, but also raising the mind to a more
high and lofty conceit. For this end have I studied
to induce a true form of versifying into our language;
for the vulgar and artificial custom of rhyming hath,
I know, deterr'd many excellent wits from the exer-
cise of English poesy." The work was published in
1602, the year after he had issued the first collection
of his lyrics. It was in answer to Campion that
Samuel Daniel wrote his admirable "Defence of
Rhyme" (1602 ; ed. 2, 1603). Daniel was puzzled,
as well he might be, that an attack on rhyme should
have been made by one "whose commendable
rhymes, albeit now himself an enemy to rhyme, have
given heretofore to the world the best notice of his
worth." It is pleasant to find Daniel testifying
to the fact that Campion was "a man of fair parts
and good reputation." Drummond reports that
Ben Jonson wrote "a Discourse of Poesy both
against Campion and Daniel;" but the discourse
was never published.

Fortunately Campion did not abandon rhyme.

His second collection, "Two Books of Airs," is
undated; but from an allusion to the death of
Prince Henry we may conclude that it was published about 1613. The first book consists of
"Divine and Moral Poems," and the second of
"Light Conceits of Lovers." In dealing with
sacred themes our English poets seldom do themselves justice; but Campion's devotional lyrics are
never stiff or awkward or vapid. "Awake, awake!
thou heavy sprite" by its impassioned fervour re-
calls Henry Vaughan. Among the moral poems
are some delightful verses ("Jack and Joan they
think no ill") in praise of a contented countryman
and his good wife. A sweeter example of an old
pastoral lyric could nowhere be found, not even in
the pages of Nicolas Breton.

"The Third and Fourth Books of Airs" are also
undated, but they cannot have been published
earlier than 1617.[1] In this collection, where all is

[1] In the dedicatory address to Sir Thomas Mounson (or
Monson), prefixed to the "Third Book," Campion writes:—

"Since now those clouds, that lately overcast
Your fame and fortune, are dispersed at last;
And now since all to you fair greetings make,
Some out of love and some for pity's sake;
Shall I but with a common style salute
Your new enlargement, or stand only mute?

good, my favourite is "Now winter nights enlarge."
Others may prefer the melodious serenade, worthy
even of Shelley, "Shall I come, sweet love, to
thee?" But there is one poem of Campion
(printed in the collection of 1601) which, for
romantic beauty, could hardly be matched outside
the sonnets of Shakespeare :—

"When thou must home to shades of underground
And there arrived, a new admired guest,
The beauteous spirits do engirt thee round,
White Iope, blithe Helen and the rest,
To hear the stories of thy finished love
From that smooth tongue whose music hell can move;
Then wilt thou speak of banqueting delights,
Of masques and revels which sweet youth did make,
Of tourneys and great challenges of knights,
And all these triumphs for thy beauty's sake ;
When thou hast told these honours done to thee,
Then tell, O tell, how thou didst murder me."

The mention of "white Iope" was suggested by
a passage of Propertius :—

———————

I, to whose trust and care you durst commit
Your pined health when art despaired of it?"
Mounson was examined in 1615 with reference to the
Overbury murder ; the warrant for his arrest was issued in
October, 1615 ; he was liberated on bail in October, 1616,
and his pardon was granted in February, 1616-17.

Mr. Barclay Squire kindly pointed out these facts to me.

For more information about Campion, see my edition of
his "Works." He was buried on 1st March, 1619-20.

"Sunt apud infernos tot millia formosarum ;
  Pulchra sit in superis, si licet, una locis,
Vobiscum est *Iope*, vobiscum candida Tyro," &c.

Campion was steeped in classical feeling : his rendering of Catullus' "Vivamus, mea Lesbia, atque amemus" ("My sweetest Lesbia, let us live and love") is, so far as it goes, delightful.

It is time that Campion should again take his rightful place among the lyric poets of England. He was, like Shelley, occasionally careless in regard to the observance of metrical exactness, and it must be owned that he had not learned the art of blotting. But his best work is singularly precious. Whoever cannot feel the witchery of such poems as "Hark, all you ladies that do sleep!" or "Thrice toss these oaken ashes in the air," is past praying for. In his own day his fame stood high. His contemporary, John Davies of Hereford, who was himself a genuine poet, though he wrote far too much and seldom did himself justice, addressed to him a sonnet which contains words of neat and appropriate praise :—

"Never did lyrics' more than happy strains,
Strained out of Art by Nature so with ease,
So purely hit the moods and various veins
Of music and her hearers as do these.
So thou canst cure the body and the mind,

Rare doctor, with thy two-fold soundest art :
Hippocrates hath taught thee the one kind,
Apollo and the Muse the other part :
And both so well that thou with both dost please,
The mind with pleasure, and the corps with ease."

Camden did not hesitate to couple his name with
the names of Spenser and Sidney; but he has
been persistently neglected by modern critics.[1]

The rare song-books of the lutenist Robert Jones,
who had a share in the Whitefriars Theatre, contain some excellent poetry. Between 1601 and
1610 he issued six musical works. One of these,
"The Muses' Garden of Delights," 1610, I have
not been able to see, as I have not discovered its
present resting-place; but in 1812 Beloe printed
some songs from it in the sixth volume of his
"Anecdotes," and I have availed myself of his
transcript. These songs (which include "How
many new years have grown old," "Once did my
thoughts both ebb and flow," and "The sea hath
many thousand sands") are so charming that I
am consumed with a desire to see the rest of the
collection. The Royal College of Music possesses

---

[1] The fact that Campion's merits are now (1896) amply
recognized is due (I venture to think) to the urgent appeal that
I made on his behalf in the original edition of this anthology ;
but it should be noted that, before my anthology appeared,
Prof. Arber had included the greater part of Campion's work
in *An English Garner.*

one unique book of Robert Jones, his " Ultimum Vale," 1608 , but many of the choicest songs in that song-book were printed in Davison's " Poetical Rhapsody." His other publications are of the highest rarity. By turns the songs are grave and gay. On one page is the warning to Love :—

> " Little boy, pretty knave, hence, I beseech you !
> For if you hit me, knave, in faith I'll breech you."

On another we read " Love winged my Hopes and taught me how to fly ") but the vain Hopes, seeking to woo the sun's fair light, were scorched with fire and drowned in woe,

> "And none but Love their woeful hap did rue,
> For Love did know that their desires were true ;
> Though Fate frowned,
> And now drowned
> They in sorrow dwell,
> It was the purest light of heaven for whose fair love they fell."

The last line is superb.

I have drawn freely from the collections of Weelkes, Morley, Farmer, Bateson, Wilbye, and others. The " Songs for the Lute, Viol, and Voice," 1606, of John Danyel (the brother and literary executor of Samuel Daniel), and Thomas Ford's "Music of Sundry Kinds," 1607, have yielded some choice verse. William Corkine, Francis Pilkington, and John Attey have not been consulted in vain; and in Thomas Vautor's "Songs of Divers Airs and Natures," 1619, I found the charming address to the owl, "Sweet Suffolk owl, so trimly dight." From William Barley's very rare "New Book of Tabliture," 1596, I have taken the sonnet, "Those eyes that set my fancy on a fire," which had previously appeared in the "Phœnix Nest," 1593. This sonnet is freely translated from Philippe Desportes; but the anonymous translator has surpassed the French poet.

As I have no technical knowledge of the subject, it would be impertinent for me to attempt to estimate the merit of the music contained in these old song-books; but I venture with all confidence to commend the poetry to the reader's attention. It must be clearly understood that the present volume does not for a moment claim to be a representative anthology of the whole wealth of Elizabethan lyrical poetry. I have conducted the reader through only one tract of those wonderful Realms of Gold. It is solely with the old song-books, the music books, that I have here dealt. Song-writing is now almost as completely a lost art as play-writing. Our poets, who ought to make "music and sweet poetry agree," leave the writing of songs to meaner hands. Contrast the poor thin wretched stuff that one hears in drawing rooms to-day with the rich full-throated songs of Campion and Dowland. O what a fall is there, my countrymen! In Elizabethan times music was "married to immortal verse." Let us hope that the present separation will not always continue.

TABLE OF FIRST LINES.

LYRICS FROM ELIZABETHAN
SONG-BOOKS.

Let well-tuned words amaze
With harmony divine.
CAMPION.

LOVE-POEMS.

From CAPTAIN TOBIAS HUME'S
*The First Part of Airs,
French, Polish, and others
together*, 1605.

FAIN would I change that note
   To which fond love hath charm'd me
Long long to sing by rote,
Fancying that that harm'd me :
Yet when this thought doth come,
" Love is the perfect sum
Of all delight,"
I have no other choice
Either for pen or voice
To sing or write.

O Love, they wrong thee much
That say thy sweet is bitter,
When thy rich fruit is such
As nothing can be sweeter.
Fair house of joy and bliss,
Where truest pleasure is,
I do adore thee ;
I know thee what thou art,
I serve thee with my heart,
And fall before thee.

H

From ROBERT JONES' *Ultimum
Vale*, 1608.   (Words by
WALTER DAVISON.)

A T her fair hands how have I grace entreated,
   With prayers oft repeated !
   Yet still my love is thwarted :
Heart, let her go, for she'll not be converted.
   Say, shall she go ?
   O, no, no, no, no, no !
She is most fair, though she be marble-hearted.

How often have my sighs declared mine anguish,
   Wherein I daily languish !
   Yet still she doth procure it :
Heart, let her go, for I cannot endure it.
   Say, shall she go ?
   O, no, no, no, no, no !
She gave the wound, and she alone must cure it.

The trickling tears that down my cheeks have flowed
   My love have often showed ;
   Yet still unkind I prove her :
Heart, let her go, for nought I do can move her.
   Say, shall she go ?
   O, no, no, no, no, no !
Though me she hate I cannot chuse but love her.

But shall I still a true affection owe[1] her,
    Which prayers, sighs, tears do show her,
    And shall she still disdain me?
Heart, let her go, if they no grace can gain me.
    Say, shall she go?
    O, no, no, no, no, no !
She made me hers, and hers she will retain me.

But if the love that hath and still doth burn me
    No love at length return me,
    Out of my thoughts I'll set her :
Heart, let her go, O heart, I pray thee, let her.
    Say, shall she go?
    O, no, no, no, no, no !
Fixed in the heart, how can the heart forget her?

But if I weep and sigh and often wail me
    Till tears, sighs, prayers fail me,
    Shall yet my love persèver ![2]
Heart, let her go, if she will right thee never.
    Say, shall she go ?
    O no, no, no, no, no !
Tears, sighs. prayers fail, but true love lasteth ever.

---

[1] This is the reading in Davison's *Poetical Rhapsody.* The
song-book reads " bear her."
[2] Old form of " persevere."

From *Two Books of Airs,* by
THOMAS CAMPION (circ.
1613).

COME, you pretty false-eyed wanton,
　Leave your crafty smiling !
Think you to escape me now
　With slipp'ry words beguiling?
No ; you mocked me th'other day ;
　When you got loose, you fled away ;
But, since I have caught you now,
　I'll clip your wings for flying :
Smoth'ring kisses fast I'll heap
　And keep you so from crying.

Sooner may you count the stars
　And number hail down-pouring,
Tell the osiers of the Thames,
　Or Goodwin sands devouring,
Than the thick-showered kisses here
　Which now thy tired lips must bear.
Such a harvest never was
　So rich and full of pleasure,
But 'tis spent as soon as reaped,
　So trustless is love's treasure.

From *Christ Church MS.* 1. 5.
49.

" A RT thou that she than whom no fairer is,
Art thou that she desire so strives to kiss ? "
 " Say I am : how then ?
  Maids may not kiss
 Such wanton-humour'd men."

" Art thou that she the world commends for wit?
Art thou so wise and makest no use of it ? "
 " Say I am : how then ?
  My wit doth teach me shun
 Such foolish foolish men."

From JOHN WILBYE'S *First Set of
English Madrigals,* 1598.

A DIEU, sweet Amaryllis !
 For since to part your will is,
O heavy, heavy tiding !
Here is for me no biding.
Yet once again, ere that I part with you,
Adieu, sweet Amaryllis ; sweet, adieu !

From THOMAS CAMPION s *Third Book of Airs* (circ. 1617).

/

COME, O come, my life's delight,
 Let me not in languor pine !
Love loves no delay ; thy sight
 The more enjoyed, the more divine :
O come, and take from me
The pain of being deprived of thee !

Thou all sweetness dost enclose,
 Like a little world of bliss ;
Beauty guards thy looks, the rose –
 In them pure and eternal is :
Come, then, and make thy flight
As swift to me as heavenly light !

From THOMAS BATESON'S *First Set of English Madrigals,* 1604.

AY me, my mistress scorns my love ;
 I fear she will most cruel prove.
I weep, I sigh, I grieve, I groan ;
Yet she regardeth not my moan.
Then, Love, adieu ! it fits not me
To weep for her that laughs at thee.

From THOMAS CAMPION'S *Third
Book of Airs* (circ. 1617).

FIRE that must flame is with apt fuel fed,
  Flowers that will thrive in sunny soil are bred :
How can a heart feel heat that no hope finds ?
Or can he love on whom no comfort shines?

Fair, I confess there's pleasure in your sight ;
Sweet, you have power, I grant, of all delight ;
But what is all to me if I have none ?
Churl that you are t'enjoy such wealth alone !

Prayers move the heavens but find no grace with you,
Yet in your looks a heavenly form I view ;
Then will I pray again, hoping to find,
As well as in your looks, heaven in your mind.

Saint of my heart, queen of my life and love,
O let my vows thy loving spirit move !
Let me no longer mourn through thy disdain,
But with one touch of grace cure all my pain !

From CAMPION and ROSSETER's
Book of Airs, 1601.

FOLLOW your saint, follow with accents sweet !
    Haste you, sad notes, fall at her flying feet !
There, wrapped in cloud of sorrow, pity move,
And tell the ravisher of my soul I perish for her love :
But, if she scorns my never-ceasing pain,
Then burst with sighing in her sight and ne'er return
        again.

All that I sang still to her praise did tend,
Still she was first, still she my songs did end ;
Yet she my love and music both doth fly,
The music that her echo is and beauty's sympathy .
Then let my notes pursue her scornful flight !
It shall suffice that they were breathed and died for
        her delight.

From ROBERT JONES *Second Book
of Songs and Airs,* 1601.

A RISE, my Thoughts, and mount you with the sun,
Call all the winds to make you speedy wings,
And to my fairest Maya see you run
And weep your last while wantonly she sings ;
Then if you cannot move her heart to pity,
Let *Oh, alas, ay me* be all your ditty.

Arise, my Thoughts, no more, if you return
Denied of grace which only you desire,
But let the sun your wings to ashes burn
And melt your passions in his quenchless fire ;
Yet, if you move fair Maya's heart to pity,
Let smiles and love and kisses be your ditty.

Arise, my Thoughts, beyond the highest star
And gently rest you in fair Maya's eye,
For that is fairer than the brightest are ;
But, if she frown to see you climb so high,
Couch in her lap, and with a moving ditty,
Of smiles and love and kisses, beg for pity.

From JOHN DOWLAND'S *First
Book of Songs or Airs,* 1597.

MY Thoughts are winged with Hopes, my Hopes
        with Love :
Mount, Love, unto the moon in clearest night,
And say, as she doth in the heavens move,
In earth so wanes and waxeth my delight :
And whisper this, but softly, in her ears,
" Hope oft doth hang the head and Trust shed tears."

And you, my Thoughts, that some mistrust do carry,
If for mistrust my mistress do you blame,
Say, though you alter, yet you do not vary,
As she doth change and yet remain the same ;
Distrust doth enter hearts, but not infect,
And Love is sweetest seasoned with Suspect.

If she for this with clouds do mask her eyes
And make the heavens dark with her disdain,
With windy sighs disperse them in the skies
Or with thy tears dissolve them into rain.
Thoughts, Hopes, and Love, return to me no more
Till Cynthia shine as she hath done before.

From ROBERT JONES' *Second Book of Songs and Airs*, 1601

L OVE winged my Hopes and taught me how to fly
 Far from base earth, but not to mount too high :
   For true pleasure
   Lives in measure,
   Which if men forsake,
Blinded they into folly run and grief for pleasure take.

But my vain Hopes, proud of their new-taught flight,
Enamoured sought to woo the sun's fair light,
   Whose rich brightness
   Moved their lightness
   To aspire so high
That all scorch'd and consumed with fire now drown'd
  in woe they lie.

And none but Love their woeful hap did rue,
For Love did know that their desires were true ;
   Though Fate frowned,
   And now drowned
   They in sorrow dwell,
It was the purest light of heaven for whose fair love
  they fell.

From JOHN DOWLAND'S *Third
and Last Book of Songs or
Airs*, 1603.

BEHOLD a wonder here !
    Love hath received his sight !
Which many hundred year [1]
Hath not beheld the light.

Such beams infused be
By Cynthia in his eyes,
As first have made him see
And then have made him wise.

Love now no more will weep
For them that laugh the while !
Nor wake for them that sleep,
Nor sigh for them that smile !

So powerful is the Beauty
That Love doth now behold,
As Love is turned to Duty
That's neither blind nor bold.

Thus Beauty shows her might
To be of double kind ;
In giving Love his sight
And striking Folly blind.

[1] Old ed. "yeares."

From JOHN DOWLAND'S *Second Book of Songs or Airs*, 1600.

I SAW my Lady weep,
　　And Sorrow proud to be advanced so
In those fair eyes where all perfections keep.
　　Her face was full of woe,
But such a woe (believe me) as wins more hearts
Than Mirth can do with her enticing parts.

　　Sorrow was there made fair,
And Passion wise ; Tears a delightful thing ;
Silence beyond all speech, a wisdom rare ;
　　She made her sighs to sing,
And all things with so sweet a sadness move
As made my heart at once both grieve and love.

　　O fairer than aught else
The world can show, leave off in time to grieve.
Enough, enough : your joyful look excels :
　　Tears kill the heart, believe.
O strive not to be excellent in woe,
Which only breeds your beauty's overthrow.

From CAMPION and ROSSETER s
Book of Airs, 1601.

FOLLOW thy fair sun, unhappy shadow !
　　Though thou be black as night,
　　And she made all of light,
Yet follow thy fair sun, unhappy shadow !

Follow her, whose light thy light depriveth !
　　Though here thou liv'st disgraced,
　　And she in heaven is placed,
Yet follow her whose light the world reviveth !

Follow those pure beams, whose beauty burneth !
　　That so have scorched thee
　　As thou still black must be
Till her kind beams thy black to brightness turneth.

Follow her, while yet her glory shineth !
　　There comes a luckless night
　　That will dim all her light ;
And this the black unhappy shade divineth.

Follow still, since so thy fates ordained !
　　The sun must have his shade,
　　Till both at once do fade,
The sun still proved, the shadow still disdained.

From ROBERT JONES' *The Muses'
Garden of Delights*, 1610.

HOW many new years have grown old
   Since first your servant old was new!
How many long hours have I told
Since first my love was vowed to you!
And yet, alas! she doth not know
Whether her servant love or no.

How many walls as white as snow,
And windows clear as any glass,
Have I conjured to tell you so,
Which faithfully performed was!
And yet you'll swear you do not know
Whether your servant love or no.

How often hath my pale lean face,
With true characters of my love,
Petitioned to you for grace,
Whom neither sighs nor tears can move!
O cruel, yet do you not know
Whether your servant love or no?

And wanting oft a better token,
I have been fain to send my heart,
Which now your cold disdain hath broken,
Nor can you heal't by any art:
O look upon't, and you shall know
Whether your servant love or no.

ヽ
From THOMAS CAMPION'S *Fourth
Book of Airs* (circ. 1617).

DEAR, if I with guile would gild a true intent,
    Heaping flatt'ries that in heart were never meant
        Easily could I then obtain
            What now in vain I force ;
        Falsehood much doth gain,
            Truth yet holds the better course.

Love forbid that through dissembling I should thrive,
Or, in praising you, myself of truth deprive !
        Let not your high thoughts debase
            A simple truth in me ;
        Great is Beauty's grace,
            Truth is yet as fair as she.

Praise is but the wind of pride if it exceeds,
Wealth prized in itself no outward value needs :
        Fair you are, and passing fair ;
            You know it, and 'tis true ;
        Yet let none despair
            But to find as fair as you.

From WILLIAM BYRD'S *Songs of*
Sundry Natures, 1589.

FROM Citheron the warlike boy is fled
   And smiling sits upon a Virgin's lap,
      Thereby to train poor misers to the trap,
Whom Beauty draws with fancy to be fed :
And when Desire with eager looks is led,
            Then from her eyes
            The arrow flies,
Feather'd with flame, arm'd with a golden head.

Her [1] careless thoughts are freed of that flame
      Wherewith her thralls are scorched to the heart:
      If Love would so, would God the enchanting dart
Might once return and burn from whence it came !
Not to deface of Beauty's work the frame,
            But by rebound
            It might be found
What secret smart I suffer by the same.

If Love be just, then just is my desire ;
      And if unjust, why is he call'd a God ?
      O God, O God, O just ! reserve thy rod
To chasten those that from thy laws retire !
But choose aright (good Love, I thee require)
            The golden head,
            Not that of lead !
Her heart is frost and must dissolve by fire.

1 Old ed. " There."
C

From ROBERT JONES' *Second Book*
of Songs and Airs, 1601.

M Y love bound me with a kiss
 That I should no longer stay ;
When I felt so sweet a bliss
 I had less power to part away:
Alas ! that women doth not know
Kisses make men loath to go.

Yes, she knows it but too well,
 For I heard when Venus' dove
In her ear did softly tell
 That kisses were the seals of love :
O muse not then though it be so,
Kisses make men loath to go.

Wherefore did she thus inflame
 My desires heat my blood,
Instantly to quench the same
 And starve whom she had given food?
I the common sense can show,
Kisses make men loath to go.

Had she bid me go at first
 It would ne'er have grieved my heart,
Hope delayed had been the worst ;
 But ah to kiss and then to part !
How deep it struck, speak, gods, you know
Kisses make men loath to go.

From THOMAS CAMPION s *Two*
Books of Airs (circ. 1613).

GIVE Beauty all her right,
      She's not to one form tied ;
Each shape yields fair delight
      Where her perfections bide :
Helen, I grant, might pleasing be,
And Ros'mond was as sweet as she

Some the quick eye commends,
      Some swelling lips [1] and red ;
Pale looks have many friends,
      Through sacred sweetness bred :
Meadows have flowers that pleasures move,
Though roses are the flowers of love.

Free beauty is not bound
      To one unmoved clime ;
She visits every ground
      And favours every time.
Let the old loves with mine compare,
My sovereign is as sweet and fair.

1 Old ed. " smelling."

From JOHN DOWLAND's *Second
Book of Songs or Airs,* 1600.

FINE knacks for ladies, cheap, choice, brave and
        new,
   Good pennyworths,—but money cannot move :
I keep a fair but for the Fair to view,—
   A beggar may be liberal of love.
Though all my wares be trash, the heart is true,
                        The heart is true.

Great gifts are guiles and look for gifts again,
   My trifles come as treasures from my mind ;
It is a precious jewel to be plain ;
   Sometimes in shell the orient'st pearls we find :
Of others take a sheaf, of me a grain !
                        Of me a grain !

Within this pack pins, points, laces, and gloves,
   And divers toys fitting a country fair,
But my heart, wherein duty serves and loves,
   Turtles and twins, court's brood, a heavenly pair—
Happy the heart that thinks of no removes !
                        Of no removes !

From JOHN BARTLET'S *Airs,*
1606.

THE Queen of Paphos, Erycine,
  In heart did rose-cheeked Adon love ;
He mortal was, but she divine,
  And oft with kisses did him move ;
With great gifts still she did him woo,
But he would never yield thereto.

Then since the Queen of Love by Love
  To love was once a subject made,
And could thereof no pleasure prove,
  By day, by night, by light or shade,
Why, being mortal, should I grieve,
Since she herself could not relieve ?

She was a goddess heavenly
  And loved a fair-faced earthly boy,
Who did contemn her deity
  And would not grant her hope of joy ;
For Love doth govern by a fate
That here plants will and there leaves hate.

But I a hapless mortal wight
  To an immortal beauty sue ;
No marvel then she loathes my sight
  Since Adon Venus would not woo.
Hence groaning sighs, mirth be my friend !
Before my life, my love shall end.

From ROBERT JONES' *The Muses
Garden of Delights,* 1610.

THE sea hath many thousand sands,
   The sun hath motes as many;
The sky is full of stars, and love
As full of woes as any :
Believe me, that do know the elf,
And make no trial by thyself.

It is in truth a pretty toy
For babes to play withal;
But O the honies of our youth
Are oft our age's gall !
Self-proof in time will make thee know
He was a prophet told thee so :

A prophet that, Cassandra-like,
Tells truth without belief;
For headstrong youth will run his race,
Although his goal be grief :
Love's martyr, when his heat is past,
Proves Care's confessor at the last.

From JOHN DOWLAND'S *First
Book of Songs and Airs*, 1597.

I F my complaints could passions move,
 Or make Love see wherein I suffer wrong;
My passions were enough to prove
 That my despairs had governed me too long.
O Love, I live and die in thee!
Thy wounds do freshly bleed in me.

Thy grief in my deep sighs still speaks,
 Yet thou dost hope when I despair;
My heart for thy unkindness breaks;
 Thou say'st thou can'st my harms repair,
And when I hope thou mak'st me hope in vain;
Yet for redress thou let'st me still complain.

Can Love be rich and yet I want?
 Is Love my judge, and yet am I condemned?
Thou plenty hast, yet me dost scant;
 Thou made a god, and yet thy power contemned!
That I do live, it is thy power;
That I desire, it is thy worth.

If Love doth make men's lives too sour,
 Let me not love, nor live henceforth!
Die shall my hopes, but not my faith,
 That you, that of my fall may hearers be,
May hear Despair which saith
" I was more true to Love than Love to me."

From THOMAS CAMPION'S *Third Book of Airs* (circ. 1617).

"MAIDS are simple," some men say,
　　" They forsooth will trust no men."
But should they men's wills obey,
　　Maids were very simple then.

Truth a rare flower now is grown,
　　Few men wear it in their hearts ;
Lovers are more easily known
　　By their follies than deserts.

Safer may we credit give
　　To a faithless wandering Jew,
Than a young man's vows believe
　　When he swears his love is true.

Love they make a poor blind child,
　　But let none trust such as he ;
Rather than to be beguiled,
　　Ever let me simple be.

From ROBERT JONES' *Musical Dream*, 1609.

IN Sherwood lived stout Robin Hood,
    An archer great, none greater,
His bow and shafts were sure and good,
    Yet Cupid's were much better ;
Robin could shoot at many a hart and miss,
Cupid at first could hit a heart of his.
    Hey, jolly Robin Hood ! ho, jolly Robin Hood !
        Love finds out me
        As well as thee,
    To follow me to the green-wood.

A noble thief was Robin Hood,
    Wise was he could deceive him ;
Yet Marian in his bravest mood
    Could of his heart bereave him :
No greater thief lies hidden under skies,
Than beauty closely lodged in women's eyes.
    Hey, jolly Robin &c.

An outlaw was this Robin Hood,
    His life free and unruly,
Yet to fair Marian bound he stood
    And love's debt paid her duly :
Whom curb of strictest law could not hold in,
Love [1] to obedience with a wink could win.
    Hey, jolly Robin &c.

1 Old ed. " Love with obeyednes and a winke could winne."

Now wend we home, stout Robin Hood,
   Leave we the woods behind us,
Love-passions must not be withstood,
   Love everywhere will find us.
I lived in field and town, and so did he ;
I got me to the woods, Love followed me.
   Hey, jolly Robin &c.

                  From JOHN WILBYE'S *Second Set*
                      of Madrigals, 1609.

L OVE not me for comely grace,
   For my pleasing eye or face,
Nor for any outward part :
No, nor for a constant heart !
For these may fail or turn to ill :
   So thou and I shall sever.
Keep therefore a true woman's eye,
And love me still, but know not why !
So hast thou the same reason still
   To doat upon me ever.

From ROBERT JONES *Ultimum
Vale or Third Book of Airs*
(1608).

NOW have I learn'd with much ado at last
   By true disdain to kill desire ;
This was the mark at which I shot so fast,
   Unto this height I did aspire :
Proud Love, now do thy worst and spare not,
For thee and all thy shafts I care not.

What hast thou left wherewith to move my mind,
   What life to quicken dead desire ?
I count thy words and oaths as light as wind,
   I feel no heat in all thy fire :
Go, change thy bow and get a stronger,
Go, break thy shafts and buy thee longer.

In vain thou bait'st thy hook with beauty's blaze,
   In vain thy wanton eyes allure ;
These are but toys for them that love to gaze,
   I know what harm thy looks procure :
Some strange conceit must be devised,
Or thou and all thy skill despised.

From Thomas Campion's *Third
Book of Airs* (circ. 1617).

AWAKE, thou spring of speaking grace ! mute rest
    becomes not thee :
The fairest women while they sleep, and pictures,
    equal be.
      O come and dwell in love's discourses !
      Old renewing, new creating.
      The words which thy rich tongue discourses
      Are not of the common rating.

Thy voice is as an Echo clear which music doth beget,
Thy speech is as an oracle which none can counter-
    feit :
      For thou alone, without offending,
        Hast obtained power of enchanting,
      And I could hear thee without ending,
        Other comfort never wanting.

Some little reason brutish lives with human glory
    share,
But language is our proper grace from which they
    severed are.
      As brutes in reason man surpasses,
        Men in speech excel each other :
      If speech be then the best of graces,
        Do it not in slumber smother.

From JOHN FARMER'S *First Set
of English Madrigals*, 1599.

O STAY, sweet love; see here the place of sporting;
   These gentle flowers smile sweetly to invite us,
And chirping birds are hitherward resorting,
   Warbling sweet notes only to delight us:
Then stay, dear Love, for, tho' thou run from me,
Run ne'er so fast, yet I will follow thee.

I thought, my love, that I should overtake you;
   Sweet heart, sit down under this shadowed tree,
And I will promise never to forsake you,
   So you will grant to me a lover's fee.
Whereat she smiled, and kindly to me said—
I never meant to live and die a maid.

From THOMAS RAVENSCROFT'S
Melismata, 1611.

THE COURTIER'S COURTSHIP TO HIS MISTRESS.

WILL ye love me, lady sweet?
   You are young, and love is meet.
Out alas! who then will sport thee?
Wanton yet in the spring:
Love is a pretty thing.
Kiss sweet as lovers do;
Prove kind to them that woo.

THE MISTRESS TO THE COURTIER.

Fie away, fie away! fie, fie, fie!
No, no, no, no, no, no, no, no, not I!
I'll live a maid till I be forty.

From THOMAS MORLEY'S *First
Book of Airs*, 1600.

THYRSIS and Milla, arm in arm together,
  In merry may-time to the green garden walked,
Where all the way they wanton riddles talked ;
The youthful boy, kissing her cheeks so rosy,
Beseech'd her there to gather him a posy.
She straight her light green silken coats uptucked,
And may for Mill and thyme for Thyrsis plucked ;
Which when she brought, he clasped her by the middle
And kiss'd her sweet, but could not read her riddle.
"Ah, fool !" with that the nymph set up a laughter,
And blush'd, and ran away, and he ran after.

From THOMAS WEELKES' *Ballets
and Madrigals*, 1598.

NOW is my Chloris fresh as May,
  Clad all in green and flowers gay.
            Fa la la !
O might I think August were near
That harvest joy might soon appear.
            Fa la la !
But she keeps May throughout the year,
And August never comes the near.[1]
            Fa la la !
Yet will I hope, though she be May,
August will come another day.
            Fa la la !

[1] Nearer.

From Thomas Ford's *Music of Sundry Kinds,* 1607.

THERE is a Lady sweet and kind,
   Was never face so pleased my mind;
I did but see her passing by,
And yet I love her till I die.

Her gesture, motion and her smiles
Her wit, her voice my heart beguiles,
Beguiles my heart, I know not why,
And yet I love her till I die.

Her free behaviour, winning looks,
Will make a Lawyer burn his books;
I touched her not, alas! not I,
And yet I love her till I die.

Had I her fast betwixt mine arms,
Judge you that think such sports were harms;
Were't any harm? no, no, fie, fie,
For I will love her till I die.

Should I remain confined there
· So long as Phœbus in his sphere,
I to request, she to deny,
Yet would I love her till I die.

Cupid is winged and doth range,
Her country so my love doth change :
But change she earth, or change she sky,
Yet will I love her till I die.

LOVE-POEMS.

From THOMAS CAMPION'S *Fourth Book of Airs* (circ. 1617).

THINK'ST thou to seduce me then with words
  that have no meaning?
Parrots so can learn to prate, our speech by pieces
  gleaning :
Nurses teach their children so about the time of
  weaning.

Learn to speak first, then to woo: to wooing much
  pertaineth :
He that courts us, wanting art, soon falters when he
  feigneth,
Looks asquint on his discourse and smiles when he
  complaineth.

Skilful anglers hide their hooks, fit baits for every
  season ;
But with crooked pins fish thou, as babes do that
  want reason :
Gudgeons only can be caught with such poor tricks of
  treason.

Ruth forgive me (if I erred) from human heart's com-
  passion,
When I laughed sometimes too much to see thy foolish
  fashion :
But, alas, who less could do that found so good occasion?

From JOHN WILBYE's *Madrigals*,
1598.

THOU art but young, thou say'st,
 And love's delight thou weigh'st not :
O, take time while thou may'st,
 Lest when thou would'st thou may'st not.

If love shall then assail thee,
 A double anguish will torment thee ;
And thou wilt wish (but wishes all will fail thee,)
  "O me ! that I were young again !" and so repent
   thee.

From CAMPION and ROSSETER's
Book of Airs, 1601.

THOU art not fair, for all thy red and white,
 For all those rosy ornaments in thee ;
Thou art not sweet, tho' made of mere delight,
 Nor fair, nor sweet—unless thou pity me.
I will not soothe thy fancies, thou shalt prove
That beauty is no beauty without love.

Yet love not me, nor seek not to allure
 My thoughts with beauty were it more divine ;
Thy smiles and kisses I cannot endure,
 I'll not be wrapped up in those arms of thine :
Now show it, if thou be a woman right,—
Embrace and kiss and love me in despite.

D

From WILLIAM BYRD'S *Psalms,
Sonnets, and Songs of Sadness
and Piety,* 1588.

THOUGH Amaryllis dance in green
       Like Fairy Queen,
       And sing full clear ;
Corinna can, with smiling, cheer.
Yet since their eyes make heart so sore,
Hey ho ! chill[1] love no more.

My sheep are lost for want of food
       And I so wood[2]
       That all the day
I sit and watch a herd-maid gay ;
Who laughs to see me sigh so sore,
Hey ho ! chill love no more.

Her loving looks, her beauty bright,
       Is such delight
       That all in vain
I love to like, and lose my gain
For her, that thanks me not therefore.
Hey ho ! chill love no more.

Ah wanton eyes ! my friendly foes
       And cause of woes,
       Your sweet desire
Breeds flames of ice, and freezing[3] fire !
Ye scorn to see me weep so sore :
Hey ho ! chill love no more.

---

[1] "Chill"—I will.   [2] Distracted.
[3] Old ed. "freeze in fire."

Love ye who list, I force him not :
Since God it wot,
The more I wail,
The less my sighs and tears prevail.
What shall I do? but say therefore,
Hey ho ! chill love no more.

From THOMAS CAMPION's *Fourth
Book of Airs* (circ. 1617).

TURN all thy thoughts to eyes,
Turn all thy hairs to ears,
Change all thy friends to spies
And all thy joys to fears ;
True love will yet be free
In spite of jealousy.

Turn darkness into day,
Conjectures into truth,
Believe what th' envious say,
Let age interpret youth :
True love will yet be free
In spite of jealousy.

Wrest every word and look,
Rack every hidden thought,
Or fish with golden hook ;
True love cannot be caught :
For that will still be free
In spite of jealousy.

From JOHN DOWLAND'S *Third and Last Book of Songs or Airs*, 1603.

WHAT poor astronomers are they,
 Take women's eyes for stars !
And set their thoughts in battle 'ray,
To fight such idle wars ;
When in the end they shall approve,
'Tis but a jest drawn out of Love.

And Love itself is but a jest
Devised by idle heads,
To catch young Fancies in the nest,
And lay them [1] in fools' beds ;
That being hatched in beauty's eyes
They may be fledged ere they be wise.

But yet it is a sport to see,
How Wit will run on wheels ;
While Will [2] cannot persuaded be,
With that which Reason feels,
That women's eyes and stars are odd
And Love is but a feigned god.

But such as will run mad with Will,
I cannot clear their sight
But leave them to their study still,
To look where is no light,
Till, time too late, we make them try
They study false Astronomy.

---

[1] Old ed. "it."   [2] Old ed. "Wit."

From THOMAS CAMPION'S *Third
Book of Airs* (circ. 1617).

NEVER love unless you can
  Bear with all the faults of man :
Men sometimes will jealous be
Though but little cause they see ;
And hang the head as discontent,
And speak what straight they will repent.

Men that but one saint adore
Make a show of love to more ;
Beauty must be scorned in none,
Though but truly served in one :
For what is courtship but disguise ?
True hearts may have dissembling eyes.

Men, when their affairs require,
Must awhile themselves retire ;
Sometimes hunt, and sometimes hawk,
And not ever sit and talk.
If these and such-like you can bear,
Then like, and love, and never fear !

From THOMAS CAMPION'S *Third
Book of Airs* (circ. 1617).

SLEEP, angry beauty, sleep and fear not me !
 For who a sleeping lion dares provoke ?
It shall suffice me here to sit and see
 Those lips shut up that never kindly spoke :
What sight can more content a lover's mind
Than beauty seeming harmless, if not kind ?

My words have charmed her, for secure she sleeps,
 Though guilty much of wrong done to my love ;
And in her slumber, see ! she close-eyed weeps :
 Dreams often more than waking passions move.
Plead, Sleep, my cause, and make her soft like thee,
That she in peace may wake and pity me.

From JOHN WILBYE'S *Second Set
of Madrigals,* 1609.

SO light is love, in matchless beauty shining,
 When he revisits Cypris' hallowed bowers,
Two feeble doves, harness'd in silken twining,
 Can draw his chariot midst the Paphian flowers.
Lightness in love ! how ill it fitteth !
So heavy on my heart he sitteth.

From THOMAS CAMPION'S *Third Book of Airs* (circ. 1617).

SILLY boy! 'tis full moon yet, thy night as day
    shines clearly ;
Had thy youth but wit to fear, thou couldst not love
    so dearly.
Shortly wilt thou mourn when all thy pleasures are
    bereaved,
Little knows he how to love that never was deceived.

This is thy first maiden-flame that triumphs yet
    unstained,
All is artless now you speak, not one word yet is
    feigned ;
All is heaven that you behold, and all your thoughts
    are blessed,
But no spring can want his fall, each Troilus hath his
    Cressid.

Thy well-ordered locks ere long shall rudely hang
    neglected,
And thy lively pleasant cheer read grief on earth
    dejected ;
Much then wilt thou blame thy Saint, that made thy
    heart so holy
And with sighs confess, in love that too much faith is
    folly.

Yet be just and constant still, Love may beget a wonder,
Not unlike a summer's frost or winter's fatal thunder :   .
He that holds his sweetheart true unto his day of dying,
Lives, of all that ever breathed, most worthy the
    envỳing.

From THOMAS FORD'S *Music of
Sundry Kinds, 1607.

SINCE first I saw your face I resolved to honour
    and renown ye ;
If now I be disdained I wish my heart had never
    known ye.
What ? I that loved and you that liked shall we begin
    to wrangle ?
No, no, no, my heart is fast, and cannot disentangle.

If I admire or praise you too much, that fault you may
    forgive me,
Or if my hands had strayed but a touch, then justly
    might you leave me.
I asked you leave, you bade me love ; is't now a time
    to chide me ?
No, no, no, I'll love you still what fortune e'er betide me.

The sun whose beams most glorious are, rejecteth no
    beholder,
And your sweet beauty past compare made my poor
    eyes the bolder :
Where beauty moves, and wit delights and signs of
    kindness bind me,
There, O there ! where'er I go I'll leave my heart
    behind me.

From WILLIAM BYRD'S *Psalms, Sonnets, and Songs,* 1588.

WHO likes to love, let him take heed !
    And wot you why?
Among the gods it is decreed
    That Love shall die ;
And every wight that takes his part
Shall forfeit each a mourning heart.

The cause is this, as I have heard :
    A sort [1] of dames,
Whose beauty he did not regard
    Nor secret flames,
Complained before the gods above
That gold corrupts the god of love.

The gods did storm to hear this news,
    And there they swore,
That sith he did such dames abuse
    He should no more
Be god of love, but that he should
Both die and forfeit all his gold.

His bow and shafts they took away
    Before his eyes,
And gave these dames a longer day
    For to devise
Who should them keep, and they be bound
That love for gold should not be found.

[1] "Sort"—company.

These ladies striving long, at last
    They did agree
To give them to a maiden chaste,
    Whom I did see,
Who with the same did pierce my breast :
Her beauty's rare, and so I rest.

From THOMAS BATESON'S First
Set of English Madrigals,
1604.

WHO prostrate lies at women's feet,
    And calls them darlings dear and sweet ;
Protesting love, and craving grace,
And praising oft a foolish face ;
Are oftentimes deceived at last,
Then catch at nought and hold it fast.

From JOHN FARMER'S First Set
of English Madrigals, 1599.

WHO would have thought that face of thine
    Had been so full of doubleness,
Or that within those chrystal eyn
    Had been so much unstableness ?
Thy face so fair, thy look so strange !
Who would have thought of such a change ?

From THOMAS CAMPION'S *Third
Book of Airs* (circ. 1617).

B E thou then my Beauty named,
    Since thy will is to be mine ;
For by that I am enflamed
    Which on all alike doth shine ;
Others may the light admire,
I only truly feel the fire.

But if lofty titles move thee,
    Challenge then a Sovereign's place ;
Say I honour when I love thee,
    Let me call thy kindness Grace :
State and Love things diverse be,
Yet will we teach them to agree.

Or if this be not sufficing,
    Be thou styled my Goddess then :
I will love thee, sacrificing ;
    In thine honour hymns I'll pen :
To be thine, what canst thou more ?
I'll love thee, serve thee, and adore.

From JOHN DOWLAND'S *Second
Book of Songs or Airs,* 1600.

A SHEPHERD in a shade his plaining made
    Of love and lover's wrong
Unto the fairest lass that trod on grass,
    And thus began his song :
"Since Love and Fortune will, I honour still
    Your fair and lovely eye :
What conquest will it be, sweet Nymph, for thee
    If I for sorrow die ?
        Restore, restore my heart again
        Which love by thy sweet looks hath slain,
        Lest that, enforced by your disdain, I sing
        ' Fie, fie, on love ! it is a foolish thing.'

" My heart where have you laid ? O cruel maid,
    To kill where you might save ?
Why have ye cast it forth as nothing worth,
    Without a tomb or grave ?
O let it be entombed and lie
    In your sweet mind and memory,
Lest I resound on every warbling stream
    ' Fie, fie on love ! that is a foolish thing.'
        Restore, restore my heart again
        Which love by thy sweet looks hath slain,
        Lest that, enforced by your disdain, I sing
        ' Fie, fie on love ! it [1] is a foolish thing.'"

            [1] Old ed. " that."

From THOMAS CAMPION's *Third Book of Airs* (circ. 1617).

THRICE toss these oaken ashes in the air,
   Thrice sit thou mute in this enchanted chair,
Then thrice-three times tie up this true love's knot,
And murmur soft " She will or she will not."

Go, burn these poisonous weeds in yon blue fire,
These screech-owl's feathers and this prickling briar,
This cypress gathered at a dead man's grave,
That all my fears and cares an end may have.

Then come, you Fairies ! dance with me a round !
Melt her hard heart with your melodious sound !
In vain are all the charms I can devise :
She hath an art to break them with her eyes.

From THOMAS BATESON's *First Set of English Madrigals,* 1604.

YOUR shining eyes and golden hair,
   Your lily-rosed lips so fair ;
Your various beauties which excel,
Men cannot choose but like them well :
Yet when for them they say they'll die,
Believe them not,—they do but lie.

From J. DANYEL's *Songs for the
Lute, Viol, and Voice,* 1606.

L ET not Chloris think, because
   She hath envassel'd me,
That her beauty can give laws
   To others that are free.
I was made to be the prey
   And booty of her eyes:
In my bosom, she may say,
   Her greatest kingdom lies.

Though others may her brow adore,
Yet more must I that therein see far more
Than any other's eyes have power to see ;
She is to me
More than to any others she can be.
I can discern more secret notes
That in the margin of her cheeks Love quotes
Than any else besides have art to read ;
No looks proceed
From those fair eyes but to me wonder breed.

O then why
Should she fly
From him to whom her sight
Doth add so much above her might ?
Why should not she
Still joy to reign in me ?

From WILLIAM BYRD'S *Psalms,
Sonnets, and Songs,* 1588.

A MBITIOUS love hath forced me to aspire
  The beauties rare which do adorn thy face ;
Thy modest life yet bridles my desire,
Whose severe law doth promise me no grace.
But what ! may Love live under any law ?
No, no, his power exceedeth man's conceit,
Of which the Gods themselves do stand in awe,
For on his frown a thousand torments wait.
Proceed then in this desperate enterprise
With good advice, and follow Love thy guide,
That leads thee to thy wished paradise.
Thy climbing thoughts this comfort take withal :
That, if it be thy foul disgrace to slide,
Thy brave attempt shall yet excuse thy fall.

From THOMAS WEELKES' *Madrigals,* 1597.

A H me ! my wonted joys forsake me,
  And deep despair doth overtake me ;
I whilome sung, but now I weep :
Thus sorrows run, when joys do creep.
I wish to live, and yet I die ;
For love hath wrought my misery.

From CAMPION and ROSSETER'S
Book of Airs, 1601.

BLAME not my cheeks, though pale with love they
    be ;
  The kindly heat unto my heart is flown
To cherish it that is dismayed by thee,
  Who art so cruel and unsteadfast grown ;
For Nature, called for by distressed hearts,
Neglects and quite forsakes the outward parts.

But they whose cheeks with careless blood are stained
  Nurse not one spark of love within their hearts ;
And, when they woo, they speak with passion feigned,
  For their fat love lies in their outward parts :
But in their breasts, where love his court should hold,
Poor Cupid sits and blows his nails for cold.

From THOMAS VAUTOR'S *Songs
of divers Airs and Natures,*
1619.

BLUSH, my rude present ; blushing, yet say this,—
    That he that sent thee meant a better thing :
Best meaners oft of their best purpose miss,
  Best runners sometimes fail to hit the ring ;
What wants in show he doth supply in mind :
Tell my sweet mistress, saint of woman-kind.

From JOHN WILBYE's *Second Set of Madrigals*, 1609.

CHANGE me, O heavens into the ruby stone
   That on my love's fair locks doth hang in gold,
Yet leave me speech to her to make my moan,
  And give me eyes her beauties to behold ;
Or if you will not make my flesh a stone,
Make her hard heart seem flesh that now seems none.

From THOMAS BATESON'S *Second Set of Madrigals*, 1618.

CAMELLA fair tripped o'er the plain,
   I followed quickly after ;
Have overtaken her I would fain,
   And kissed her when I caught her.
But hope being passed her to obtain,
   " Camella ! " loud I call :
She answered me with great disdain,
   " I will not kiss at all."

E

From ROBERT JONES' *First Book*
of Songs and Airs, 1601.

IF fathers knew but how to leave
    Their children wit as they do wealth,
And could constrain them to receive
    That physic which brings perfect health,
The world would not admiring stand
A woman's face and woman's hand.

Women confess they must obey,
    We men will needs be servants still ;
We kiss their hands, and what they say
    We must commend, be't ne'er so ill :
Thus we, like fools, admiring stand
Her pretty foot and pretty hand.

We blame their pride, which we increase
    By making mountains of a mouse ;
We praise because we know we please ;
    Poor women are too credulous
To think that we admiring stand
Or foot, or face, or foolish hand.

From ROBERT JONES' *Ultimum Vale,* 1608.

DO not, O do not prize thy beauty at too high a rate,
  Love to be loved whilst thou art lovely, lest thou
    love too late ;
  Frowns print wrinkles in thy brows
  At which spiteful age doth smile
  Women in their froward vows
  Glorying to beguile.

Wert thou the only world's admired thou canst love
      but one,
And many have before been loved, thou art not loved
    alone :
  Couldst thou speak with heavenly grace,
  Sappho might with thee compare ;
  Blush the roses in thy face,
  Rosamond was as fair.

Pride is the canker that consumeth beauty in her prime,
They that delight in long debating feel the curse of
      time :
  All things with the time do change,
  That will not the time obey ;
  Some even to themselves seem strange
  Thorough their own delay.

From JOHN DOWLAND'S *A Pilgrim's Solace*, 1612.

DISDAIN me still that I may ever love,
For who his love enjoys can love no more :
The war once past, with ease men cowards prove,
And ships returned do rot upon the shore :
And though thou frown, I'll say thou art most fair,
And still I'll love, though still I must despair.

As heat to life, so is desire to love,
And these once quenched both life and love are gone :
Let not my sighs nor tears thy virtue move,
Like baser metals do not melt too soon :
Laugh at my woes although I ever mourn ;
Love surfeits with reward, his nurse is scorn.

From ALFONSO FERRABOSCO'S
Airs, 1609.

FAIN I would, but oh I dare not,
Speak my thoughts at full to praise her :
"Speak the best," cries Love, "and spare not ;
Thy speech can no higher raise her :
Thy speech than thy thoughts are lower,
Yet thy thoughts doth not half know her."

From THOMAS CAMPION'S *Two
Books of Airs* (circ. 1613.)

HARDEN now thy tired heart with more than
flinty rage !
Ne'er let her false tears henceforth thy constant grief
assuage !
Once true happy days thou saw'st, when she stood firm
and kind ;
Both as one then lived, and held one ear, one tongue,
one mind :
But now those bright hours be fled and never may
return :
What then remains but her untruths to mourn !

Silly trait'ress, who shall now thy careless tresses
place?
Who thy pretty talk supply? whose ear thy music
grace?
Who shall thy bright eyes admire, what lips triumph
with thine?
Day by day who'll visit thee and say " Th'art only
mine"?
Such a time there was, God wot, but such shall never
be.
Too oft, I fear, thou wilt remember me.

From THOMAS CAMPION'S *Fourth
Book of Airs* (circ. 1617).

H ER fair inflaming eyes,
　　Chief authors of my cares,
I prayed in humblest wise
　　With grace to view my tears :
They beheld me broad awake,
But, alas, no ruth would take.

Her lips with kisses rich,
　　And words of fair delight,
I fairly did beseech
　　To pity my sad plight :
But a voice from them broke forth,
As a whirlwind from the north.

Then to her hands I fled,
　　That can give heart and all ;
To them I long did plead,
　　And loud for pity call :
But, alas, they put me off
With a touch worse than a scoff.

So back I straight return'd,
　　And at her breast I knock'd,
Where long in vain I mourn'd,
　　Her heart so fast was lock'd :
Not a word could passage find,
For a rock enclosed her mind.

Then down my prayers made way
  To those most comely parts
That make her fly or stay,
  As they affect deserts :
But her angry feet, thus moved,
Fled with all the parts I loved.

Yet fled they not so fast
  As her enraged mind :
Still did I after haste,
  Still was I left behind ;
Till I found 'twas to no end
With a spirit to contend.

From THOMAS BATESON S *Second*
Set of Madrigals, 1618.

HER hair the net of golden wire,
  Wherein my heart, led by my wandering eyes,
So fast entangled is that in no wise
It can, nor will, again retire ;
But rather will in that sweet bondage die
Than break one hair to gain her liberty.

From JOHN BARTLET'S *Airs*,
1606.

I HEARD of late that Love was fall'n asleep ;
   Too late, alas ! I find it was not so :
Methought I saw the little villain weep,
   But thief ! he laughs at them that wail in woe :
I dream'd his bow was broke and he was slain
But lo ! awaked, I see all whole again.

His blinking eyes will ever be awake,
   His idle head is full of laughing toys,
His bow and shafts are tickle things to take,
   It is no meddling with such apish boys ;
For they shall find, that in his fetters fall,
Love is a deadly thing to deal withal.

Yet where the wretch doth take a happy vein,
   It is the kindest worm that ever was ;
But let him catch a coy conceit again,
   In frantic fits he doth a fury pass :
So that, in sum, who hopes of happy joy,
Take heed of Love, it is a parlous boy.

From ROBERT JONES *The Muses
Garden of Delights*, 1610.

J OY in thy hope, the earnest of thy love,
   For so thou mayst enjoy thy heart's desire :
True hopes things absent do as present prove,
And keep alive love's still-renewing fire.

But of thy hope let silence be the tongue,
And secresy the heart of loving fire ;
For hopes revealed may thy hopes prolong
Or cut them off in prime-time of desire.

Sweet are those hopes that do themselves enjoy,
As vowed to themselves to live and die ;
Sweetest those joys and freest from annoy
That waken not the eye of jealousy.

L'Envoy.
Thy love is not thy love if not thine own,
And so it is not if it once be known.

From MARTIN PEERSON'S *Private Music,* 1620.

He.[1]   I S not that my fancy's Queen,
              In the brightness of her rays
              Passing summer's cheerest days,
         That comes tripping o'er the green ?

She.   Is[2] not that my shepherd swain
              Sprightly clad in lovely blue,
              Fairest of the fairest crew,
         That comes gliding o'er the plain ?

Both. It is my love, it is my love,
              And thus and thus we meet,
              And thus and thus we greet,
         Happier than the gods above :
         Meeting may we love for ever,
         Ever love and never sever !

[1] There are no prefixes in old ed.
[2] The second stanza is printed in old ed. as part of another song.

From THOMAS CAMPION s *Third
Book of Airs* (circ. 1617).

IF love loves truth then women do not love ;
　Their passions all are but dissembled shows :
Now kind and free of favour if they prove,
Their kindness straight a tempest overthrows.
Then as a seaman the poor lover fares ;
The storm drowns him ere he can drown his cares.

But why accuse I women that deceive ?
Blame then the foxes for their subtle wile !
They first from Nature did their craft receive ;
It is a woman's nature to beguile.
Yet some, I grant, in loving steadfast grow ;
But such by use are made, not Nature, so.

O why had Nature power at once to frame
Deceit and Beauty, traitors both to Love ?
O would Deceit had died when Beauty came
With her divineness every heart to move !
Yet do we rather wish, whate'er befall,
To have fair women false than none at all.

From CAMPION and ROSSETER s
Book of Airs, 1601.

IF she forsake me, I must die :
  Shall I tell her so ?
Alas, then straight will she reply,
  " No, no, no, no, no ! "
If I disclose my desperate state,
She will but make sport thereat,
  And more unrelenting grow.

What heart can long such pains abide ?
  Fie upon this love !
I would adventure far and wide,
  If it would remove ;
But love will still my steps pursue,
I cannot his ways eschew :
  Thus still helpless hopes I prove.

I do my love in lines commend,
  But, alas, in vain ;
The costly gifts that I do send,
  She returns again :
Thus still is my despair procured,
And her malice more assured :
  Then come, death, and end my pain !

From THOMAS BATESON'S *Second
Set of Madrigals*, 1618.

M Y mistress after service due
     Demanded if indeed my love were true.
I said it was ; then she replied,
That I must hate
Whom she defied,
And so myself above the rest,
Whom she (she swore) did most of all detest.
In sooth, said I, you see I hate myself,
Who sets my love on such a peevish elf.

From MARTIN PEERSON'S *Private Music*, 1620.

L OVE her no more, herself she doth not love :
     Shame and the blackest clouds of night
     Hide her for ever from thy sight.
O day, why do thy beams in her eyes move ?
     Fly her, dear honoured friend, do so ;
     She'll be the cause of much much woe.
          Alas, she will undo thee,
          Her love is fatal to thee :
     Curse her then and go !

From THOMAS CAMPION'S *Fourth
Books of Airs* (circ. 1617).

L OVE me or not, love her I must or die;
Leave me or not, follow her needs must I.
O that her grace would my wish'd comforts give !
How rich in her, how happy should I live !

All my desire, all my delight should be
Her to enjoy, her to unite to me ;
Envy should cease, her would I love alone :
Who loves by looks is seldom true to one.

Could I enchant, and that it lawful were,
Her would I charm softly that none should hear ;
But love enforced rarely yields firm content :
So would I love that neither should repent.

From THOMAS MORLEY'S *Plain
and Easy Introduction to
Practical Music*, 1597.

S LEEP, O sleep, fond fancy,
My head, alas, thou tirest
With false delight of that which thou desirest.
Sleep, I say, fond fancy,
And leave my thoughts molesting
Thy master's head hath need of sleep and resting.

From THOMAS CAMPION's *Fourth
Book of Airs* (circ. 1617).

O LOVE, where are thy shafts, thy quiver, and thy
bow?
Shall my wounds only weep and he ungaged go?
Be just and strike him too that dares contemn thee so.

No eyes are like to thine, though men suppose thee
blind,
So fair they level when the mark they list to find ;
Then strike, O strike the heart that bears the cruel
mind.

Is my fond sight deceived, or do I Cupid spy
Close aiming at his breast by whom despised I die ?
Shoot home, sweet Love, and wound him that he may
not fly.

O then we both will sit in some unhaunted shade
And heal each other's wound which Love hath justly
made ;
O hope, O thought too vain, how quickly dost thou
fade !

At large he wanders still, his heart is free from pain,
While secret sighs I spend and tears, but all in vain :
Yet, Love, thou knowest, by right I should not thus
complain.

From *Christ Church MS.* 1. 5. 49.
(Music by ALFONSO FERRA-
BOSCO.)

DAPHNIS came on a summer's day
   Where fair Phillis sleeping lay,
With breast half naked bare :
He ran and gathered stores of lilies,
Wherewith he covered his fair Phillis,
She being nought aware.
Fond youth, why dost thou mar
Those lily-bowers and lose the pain !
Her lily breast doth stain
All flowers and lilies far.

From JOHN WILBYE'S.*Madrigals,*
1598.

LADY, when I behold the roses sprouting,
   Which clad in damask mantles deck the arbours,
   And then behold your lips where sweet love
      harbours,
My eyes present me with a double doubting :
For viewing both alike, hardly my mind supposes
Whether the roses be your lips or your lips the roses.

From ROBERT JONES' *The Muses'*
Garden of Delights, 1610.

ONCE did my thoughts both ebb and flow,
　　As passion did them move ;
Once did I hope, straight fear again,—
　　And then I was in love.

Once did I waking spend the night,
　　And tell how many minutes move.
Once did I wishing waste the day,—
　　And then I was in love.

Once, by my carving true love's knot,
　　The weeping trees did prove
That wounds and tears were both our lot,—
　　And then I was in love.

Once did I breathe another's breath
　　And in my mistress move,
Once was I not mine own at all,—
　　And then I was in love.

Once wore I bracelets made of hair,
　　And collars did approve,
Once wore my clothes made out of wax,[1]—
　　And then I was in love.

Once did I sonnet to my saint,
　　My soul in numbers move,
Once did I tell a thousand lies,—
　　And then I was in love.

[1] " Clothes made out of wax "—clothes of faultless fit.

F

Once in my ear did dangling hang
  A little turtle-dove,
Once, in a word, I was a fool,—
  And then I was in love.

From MARTIN PEERSON'S *Private Music*, 1620.

"OPEN the door! Who's there within?
    The fairest of thy mother's kin,
O come, come, come abroad
And hear the shrill birds sing,
  The air with tunes that load !
It is too soon to go to rest,
The sun not midway yet to west :
  The day doth miss thee
And will not part until it kiss thee."

"Were I as fair as you pretend,
Yet to an unknown, seld-seen [1] friend
I dare not ope the door :
  To hear the sweet birds sing
  Oft proves a dangerous thing.
The sun may run his wonted race
And yet not gaze on my poor face ;
  The day may miss me :
Therefore depart, you shall not kiss me."

[1] *i.e.*, seldom seen.

From JOHN DANYEL'S *Songs for
the Lute, Viol, and Voice*,
1606. (Words by SAMUEL
DANIEL.)

TIME, cruel Time, canst thou subdue that brow
    That conquers all but thee, and thee too stays,
As if she were exempt from scythe or bow,
    From Love or Years, unsubject to decays ?

Or art thou grown in league with those fair eyes
    That they might help thee to consume our days ?
Or dost thou love her for her cruelties,
    Being merciless like thee, that no man weighs ?

Then do so still, although she makes no 'steem
    Of days nor years, but lets them run in vain :
Hold still thy swift-wing'd hours, that wond'ring seem
    To gaze on her, even to turn back again.

And do so still, although she nothing cares :
    Do as I do, love her although unkind :
Hold still, yet O ! I fear at unawares
    Thou wilt beguile her though thou seem'st so kind.

LOVE-POEMS.

From WILLIAM BARLEY'S *New
Book of Tabliture*, 1596.

THOSE eyes that set my fancy on a fire,
    Those crisped hairs that hold my heart in chains,
Those dainty hands which conquered my desire,
    That wit which of my thoughts doth hold the reins :
Those eyes for clearness doth the stars surpass,
    Those hairs obscure the brightness of the sun,
Those hands more white than ever ivory was,
    That wit even to the skies hath glory won.
O eyes that pierce our hearts without remorse !
    O hairs of right that wear a royal crown !
O hands that conquer more than Cæsar's force !
    O wit that turns huge kingdoms upside down !
Then, Love, be judge, what heart may therewith stand
Such eyes, such hair, such wit, and such a hand ? [1]

From GEORGE KIRBYE's *First Set
of English Madrigals*, 1597.

AH sweet, alas ! when first I saw those eyes,
    Those eyes so rich with crystal majesty,
Their wounding beauty gan [2] to tyrannise
    And made mine eyes bleed tears full plenteously :
I felt the wound, yet feared I not the deed,
Till ah ! I found my tears did inward bleed.

---

[1] In the Song-book ll. 13-14 are printed out of their place, after
l. 4.   They are rightly placed at the end of the sonnet in *The
Phœnix Nest.* (The Song-book reads " Such eyes, such head.")
  [2] Old ed. " gan (*then*) to tyrannyze."

From THOMAS CAMPION's *Third
Book of Airs* (circ. 1617).

IF thou long'st so much to learn, sweet boy, what
'tis to love,
Do but fix thy thoughts on me and thou shalt quickly
prove :
　　　Little suit at first shall win
　　　　Way to thy abashed desire,
　　　But then will I hedge thee in,
　　　　Salamander-like, with fire.

With thee dance I will, and sing, and thy fond dal-
liance bear ;
We the grovy hills will climb and play the wantons
there ;
　　　Other whiles we'll gather flowers,
　　　　Lying dallying on the grass ;
　　　And thus our delightful hours,
　　　　Full of waking dreams, shall pass.

When thy joys were thus at height, my love should
turn from thee,
Old acquaintance then should grow as strange, as
strange might be :
　　　Twenty rivals thou shouldst find,
　　　　Breaking all their hearts for me,
　　　While to all I'll prove more kind
　　　　And more forward than to thee.

Thus thy silly youth, enraged, would soon my love defy,
But, alas, poor soul, too late ! clipt wings can never fly.
   Those sweet hours which we had past,
      Called to thy mind, thy heart would burn ;
   And couldst thou fly ne'er so fast,
      They would make thee straight return.

From THOMAS CAMPION'S *Third
Book of Airs* (circ. 1617).

SHALL I come, sweet Love, to thee
    When the evening beams are set ?
Shall I not excluded be,
    Will you find no feigned let ?
Let me not, for pity, more
Tell the long hours at your door.

Who can tell what thief or foe,
    In the covert of the night,
For his prey will work my woe,
    Or through wicked foul despite ?
So may I die unredrest
Ere my long love be possest.

But to let such dangers pass,
    Which a lover's thoughts disdain,
'Tis enough in such a place
    To attend love's joys in vain :
Do not mock me in thy bed,
While these cold nights freeze me dead.

From *Musica Transalpina. The Second Book of Madrigals,* 1597.

SO saith my fair and beautiful Lycoris,
 When now and then she talketh
With me of Love :
" Love is a sprite that walketh,
That soars and flies,
And none alive can hold him,
Nor touch him, nor behold him."
Yet when her eye she turneth,
I spy where he sojourneth :
In her eyes there he flies,
But none can catch him
Till from her lips he fetch him.

From JOHN WILBYE'S *Madrigals,* 1598.

THUS saith my Chloris bright
 When we of love sit down and talk together :—
" Beware of Love, dear ; Love is a walking sprite,
        And Love is this and that
        And, O, I know not what,
And comes and goes again I wot not whether." [1]
No, no, these are but bugs [2] to breed amazing,
For in her eyes I saw his torch-light blazing."

[1] An old form of *whither*.   [2] Bugbears.

From WILLIAM BYRD'S *Songs of
Sundry Natures*, 1589.

WHEN younglings first on Cupid fix their sight,
    And see him naked, blindfold, and a boy,
Though bow and shafts and firebrand be his might,
    Yet ween they he can work them none annoy ;
And therefore with his purple wings they play,
    For glorious seemeth love though light as feather,
And when they have done they ween to scape away,
    For blind men, say they, shoot they know not
        whether.[1]
But when by proof they find that he did see,
    And that his wound did rather dim their sight,
They wonder more how such a lad as he
    Should be of such surpassing power and might.
But ants have galls, so hath the bee his sting :
Then shield me heavens, from such a subtle thing !

From WILLIAM BYRD'S *Psalms,
Songs, and Sonnets*, 1611.

CROWNED with flowers I saw fair Amaryllis
    By Thyrsis sit, hard by a fount of crystal,
And with her hand more white than snow or lilies,
    On sand she wrote *My faith shall be immortal:*
And suddenly a storm of wind and weather
Blew all her faith and sand away together.

[1] i.e., whither.

From THOMAS FORD's *Music of
Sundry Kinds,* 1607.

HOW shall I then describe my Love?
    When all men's skilful art
Is far inferior to her worth,
    To praise the unworthiest part.

She's chaste in looks, mild in her speech,
    In actions all discreet,
Of nature loving, pleasing most,
    In virtue all complete.

And for her voice a Philomel,
    Her lips may all lips scorn ;
No sun more clear than is her eye,
    In brightest summer morn.

A mind wherein all virtues rest
    And take delight to be,
And where all virtues graft themselves
    In that most fruitful tree :

A tree that India doth not yield,
    Nor ever yet was seen,
Where buds of virtue always spring,
    And all the year grow green.

That country's blest wherein she grows,
    And happy is that rock
From whence she springs : but happiest he
    That grafts in such a stock.

From JOHN DOWLAND'S *Second
Book of Songs and Airs,* 1600.

TOSS not my soul, O Love, 'twixt hope and
      fear !
   Show me some ground where I may firmly stand,
Or surely fall ! I care not which appear,
   So one will close me in a certain band.
When once of ill the uttermost is known,
The strength of sorrow quite is overthrown.

Take me, Assurance, to thy blissful hold !
   Or thou Despair, unto thy darkest cell !
Each hath full rest : the one, in joys enroll'd ;
   Th' other, in that he fears no more, is well.
When once the uttermost of ill is known,
The strength of sorrow quite is overthrown

From THOMAS MORLEY'S *Canzonets,* 1593.

DO you not know how Love lost first his seeing ?
      Because with me once gazing
On those fair eyes where all powers have their being,
She with her beauty blazing,
Which death might have revived,
Him of his sight and me of heart deprived.

From THOMAS CAMPION'S *Third Book of Airs* (circ. 1617).

WERE my heart as some men's are, thy errors
would not move me,
But thy faults I curious find and speak because I love
thee :
Patience is a thing divine, and far, I grant, above me.

Foes sometimes befriend us more, our blacker deeds
objecting,
Than th' obsequious bosom-guest with false respect
affecting :
Friendship is the Glass of Truth, our hidden stains
detecting.

While I use of eyes enjoy and inward light of reason,
Thy observer will I be and censor, but in season :
Hidden mischief to conceal in state and love is treason

From THOMAS MORLEY'S *Madrigals,* 1594.

O SWEET, alas, what say you?
Ay me, that faces discloses
The scarlet blush of sweet vermilion roses.
And yet, alas, I know not
If such a crimson staining
Be for love or disdaining ;
But if of love it grow not,
Be it disdain conceived
To see us of love's fruits so long bereaved.

From JOHN DOWLAND'S *Third
and Last Book of Songs or
Airs*, 1603.

WEEP you no more, sad fountains ;
  What need you flow so fast ?
Look how the snowy mountains
  Heaven's sun doth gently waste !
But my sun's heavenly eyes,
  View not your weeping,
  That now lies sleeping
Softly, now softly lies
       Sleeping.

Sleep is a reconciling,
  A rest that peace begets ;
Doth not the sun rise smiling
  When fair at ev'n he sets ?
Rest you then, rest, sad eyes !
  Melt not in weeping,
  While she lies sleeping,
Softly, now softly lies
       Sleeping.

From WILLIAM BYRD'S *Songs of Sundry Natures*, 1589.

WOUNDED I am, and dare not seek relief
    For this new stroke unseen but not unfelt :
No blood nor bruise is witness of my grief,
  But sighs and tears wherewith I mourn and melt.
If I complain, my witness is suspect ;
  If I contain, with cares I am undone :
Sit still and die, tell truth and be reject :
  O hateful choice that sorrow cannot shun !
Yet of us twain whose loss shall be the less,
  Mine of my life or you of your good name ?
Light is my death, regarding my distress,
  But your offence cries out to your defame,
" A virgin fair hath slain, for lack of grace,
The man that made an idol of her face ! "

From CAMPION and ROSSETER'S
Book of Airs, 1601.

I F I urge my kind desires,
    She unkind, doth them reject,
Women's hearts are painted fires,
    To deceive them that affect.
I alone, love's fires include :
She, alone, doth them delude.

She hath often vowed her love :
    But alas no fruit I find.
That her fires are false I prove,
    Yet in her no fault I find :
I was thus unhappy born,
And ordained to be her scorn.

Yet, if human care or pain
    May the heavenly order change,
She will hate her own disdain,
    And repent she was so strange ·
For a truer heart than I,
Never lived, nor loved to die.

From THOMAS CAMPION's *Third Book of Airs* (circ. 1617).

WHAT is it all that men possess, among themselves conversing?
Wealth or fame or some such boast, scarce worthy the
rehearsing.
Women only are men's good, with them in love conversing.

If weary, they prepare us rest; if sick, their hand
attends us;
When with grief our hearts are prest, their comfort
best befriends us;
Sweet or sour, they willing go to share what fortune
sends us.

What pretty babes with pain they bear, our name and
form presenting!
What we get how wise they keep, by sparing wants
preventing!
Sorting all their household cares to our observed contenting!

All this, of whose large use I sing, in two words is
expressed:
Good Wife is the good I praise, if by good men
possessed;
Bad with bad in ill suit well, but good with good live
blessed.

From THOMAS CAMPION'S *Fourth
Book of Airs* (circ. 1617).

THERE is a garden in her face
    Where roses and white lilies grow ;
A heavenly paradise is that place
Wherein all pleasant fruits do flow.
        There cherries grow which none may buy,
        Till " Cherry ripe " themselves do cry.

Those cherries fairly do enclose
Of orient pearl a double row,
Which when her lovely laughter shows,
They look like rose-buds filled with snow ;
        Yet them nor peer nor prince can buy,
        Till " Cherry ripe " themselves do cry.

Her eyes like angels watch them still,
Her brows like bended bows do stand,
Threatening with piercing frowns to kill
All that attempt, with eye or hand,
        Those sacred cherries to come nigh
        Till " Cherry ripe " themselves do cry.

From JOHN WILBYE'S *Second Set
of Madrigals,* 1609.

WHERE most my thoughts, there least mine eye
     is striking ;
 Where least I come there most my heart abideth ;
Where most I love I never show my liking ; '
From what my mind doth hold my body slideth ;
I show least care where most my care dependeth ;
A coy regard where most my soul attendeth.

Despiteful thus unto myself I languish,
    And in disdain myself from joy I banish.
These secret thoughts enwrap me so in anguish
    That life, I hope, will soon from body vanish,
And to some rest will quickly be conveyed
That on no joy, while so I lived, hath stayed.

From FRANCIS PILKINGTON'S
*First Set of Madrigals, and
Pastorals,* 1613.

POUR forth, mine eyes, the fountains of your tears ;
    Break, heart, and die, for now no hope appears ;
Hope, upon which before my thoughts were fed.
Hath left me quite forlorn and from me fled.
Yet, see, she smiles ! O see, some hope appears !
Hold. heart, and live ; mine eyes, cease off your tears.

G

From ROBERT JONES' *Ultimum*
Vale or Third Book of Airs
(1608).

OFT have I mused the cause to find
 Why Love in lady's eyes should dwell ;
I thought, because himself was blind,
 He look'd that they should guide him well :
And sure his hope but seldom fails,
For Love by ladies' eyes prevails.

But time at last hath taught me wit,
 Although I bought my wit full dear ;
For by her eyes my heart is hit,
 Deep is the wound though none appear :
Their glancing beams as darts he throws,
And sure he hath no shafts but those.

I mused to see their eyes so bright,
 And little thought they had been fire ;
I gazed upon them with delight,
 But that delight hath bred desire :
What better place can Love desire
Than that where grow both shafts and fire?

From ROBERT JONES' *First Book*
of Songs and Airs, 1601.

ONCE did I love and yet I live,
　　Though love and truth be now forgotten ;
Then did I joy, now do I grieve
　That holy vows must now be broken.

Hers be the blame that caused it so,
　Mine be the grief though it be mickle ; [1]
She shall have shame, I cause to know
　What 'tis to love a dame so fickle.

Love her that list, I am content
　For that chameleon-like she changeth,
Yielding such mists as may prevent
　My sight to view her when she rangeth.

Let him not vaunt that gains my loss,
　For when that he and time hath proved her,
She may him bring to Weeping-Cross :
　I say no more, because I loved her.

[1] Old ed. "little."

From THOMAS CAMPION's *Third Book of Airs* (circ. 1617).

O SWEET delight, O more than human bliss,
  With her to live that ever loving is !
To hear her speak whose words are so well placed
That she by them, as they in her are graced !
Those looks to view that feast the viewer's eye,
How blest is he that may so live and die !

Such love as this the Golden Times did know,
When all did reap, yet none took care to sow ;
Such love as this an endless summer makes,
And all distaste from frail affection takes.
So loved, so blest in my beloved am I :
Which till their eyes ache, let iron men envy !

From THOMAS WEELKES' *Madrigals,* 1597.

NOW every tree renews his summer's green,
  Why is your heart in winter's garments clad ?
Your beauty says my love is summer's queen,
  But your cold love like winter makes me sad :
Then either spring with buds of love again
Or else congeal my thoughts with your disdain.

From WILLIAM BYRD'S *Songs of
Sundry Natures*, 1589.

UPON a summer's day Love went to swim,
   And cast himself into a sea of tears ;
The clouds called in their light, and heaven waxed dim,
   And sighs did raise a tempest, causing fears ;
The naked boy could not so wield his arms,
   But that the waves were masters of his might,
And threatened him to work far greater harms
   If he devised not to scape by flight :
Then for a boat his quiver stood instead,
   His bow unbent did serve him for a mast,
Whereby to sail his cloth of veil he spread,
   His shafts for oars on either board he cast :
From shipwreck safe this wag got thus to shore,
And sware to bathe in lovers' tears no more.

From THOMAS CAMPION'S *Two
Books of Airs* (circ. 1613).

VAIN men ! whose follies make a god of love,
   Whose blindness beauty doth immortal deem,
Praise not what you desire, but what you prove ;
   Count those things good that are, not those that
      seem :
I cannot call her true, that's false to me,
Nor make of women, more than women be.

How fair an entrance breaks the way to love !
   How rich the golden hope, and gay delight !
What heart cannot a modest beauty move ?
   Who, seeing clear day once, will dream of night ?
She seemed a saint, that brake her faith with me ;
But proved a woman, as all other be.

So bitter is their sweet that True Content
   Unhappy men in them may never find :
Ah ! but without them, none. Both must concent,[1]
   Else uncouth are the joys of either kind.
Let us then praise their good, forget their ill !
Men must be men, and women women still.

    [1] Harmonise, accord. (Old ed. " consent.")

From THOMAS MORLEY'S *Canso-
nets,* 1593.

SEE, see, mine own sweet jewel,
What I have for my darling :
A robin red-breast and a starling.
These I give both in hope to move thee ;
Yet thou say'st I do not love thee.

From JOHN WILBYE'S *Madrigals,*
1598.

WHAT needeth all this travail and turmoiling,
Short'ning the life's sweet pleasure
To seek this far-fetched treasure
In those hot climates under Phœbus broiling ?

O fools, can you not see a traffic nearer
In my sweet lady's face, where Nature showeth
Whatever treasure eye sees or heart knoweth ?
Rubies and diamonds dainty
And orient pearls such plenty,
Coral and ambergreece sweeter and dearer
Than which the South Seas or Moluccas lend us,
Or either Indies, East or West, do send us !

From Thomas Weelkes' *Madrigals of Six Parts*, 1600.

THULE, the period of cosmography,
    Doth vaunt of Hecla, whose sulphureous fire
Doth melt the frozen clime and thaw the sky,
    Trinacrian Aetna's flames ascend not higher :
These things seem wondrous, yet more wondrous I,
Whose heart with fear doth freeze, with love doth fry.

The Andalusian merchant, that returns
    Laden with cochineal and china dishes,
Reports in Spain how strangely Fogo burns
    Amidst an ocean full of flying fishes :
These things seem wondrous, yet more wondrous I,
Whose heart with fear doth freeze, with love doth fry.

From   Francis   Pilkinton's
First Set of Madrigals, 1613.

HAVE I found her ? O rich finding !
    Goddess-like for to behold,
Her fair tresses seemly binding
    In a chain of pearl and gold.
Chain me, chain me, O most fair,
Chain me to thee with that hair !

From MARTIN PEERSON'S *Private Music,* 1620.

CAN a maid that is well bred,
   Hath a blush so lovely red,
Modest looks, wise, mild, discreet,
And a nature passing sweet,

Break her promise, untrue prove,
On a sudden change her love,
Or be won e'er to neglect
Him to whom she vowed respect?

Such a maid, alas! I know:
O that weeds 'mongst corn should grow!
Or a rose should prickles have,
Wounding where she ought to save!

I, that did her parts extol,
Will my lavish tongue control:
Outward parts do blind the eyes,
Gall in golden pills oft lies.

Reason, wake, and sleep no more,
Land upon some safer shore;
Think on her and be afraid
Of a faithless fickle maid.

Of a faithless fickle maid,
Thus true love is still betrayed:
Yet it is some ease to sing
That a maid is light of wing.

From ROBERT JONES' *The Muses
Garden of Delights*, 1610.

SOFT, Cupid, soft, there is no haste,
  For all unkindness gone and past :
Since thou wilt needs forsake me so,
Let us part friends before thou go.

Still shalt thou have my heart to use,—
When [1] I cannot otherwise chuse :
My life thou mayst command sans doubt,
Command, I say,—and go without.

And if that I do ever prove
False and unkind to gentle Love,
I'll not desire to live a day
Nor any longer—than I may.

I'll daily bless the little god,—
But not without a smarting rod.
Wilt thou still unkindly leave me ?
Now I pray God,—all ill go with thee !

  [1] Qy. " When otherwise I cannot chuse " ?

From JOHN DOWLAND'S *First Book of Songs or Airs*, 1597. (Words by FULKEGREVILLE, LORD BROOKE.)

WHOEVER thinks or hopes of love for love,
    Or who beloved in Cupid's laws doth glory,
Who joys in vows or vows not to remove,
Who by this light god hath not been made sorry,—
Let him see me, eclipsed from my sun,
With dark clouds of an earth quite overrun.

Who thinks that sorrows felt, desires hidden,
Or humble faith in constant honour armed,
Can keep love from the fruit that is forbidden ;
Who thinks that change is by entreaty charmed,—
Looking on me, let him know love's delights
Are treasures hid in caves but kept by sprites.

From JOHN DANYEL'S *Songs for the Lute, Viol, and Voice,* 1606.

WHY canst thou not, as others do,
    Look on me with unwounding eyes ?
And yet look sweet, but yet not so ;
    Smile, but not in killing wise ;
Arm not thy graces to confound ;
Only look, but do not wound.

Why should mine eyes see more in you
   Than they can see in all the rest?
For I can others' beauties view,
   And not find my heart opprest.
O be as others are to me,
Or let me be more to thee.

From THOMAS GREAVES' *Songs
of Sundry Kinds,* 1604.

YE bubbling springs that gentle music makes
   To lovers' plaints with heart-sore throbs immixed,
When as my dear this way her pleasure takes,
   Tell her with tears how firm my love is fixed;
And, Philomel, report my timerous fears,
And, echo, sound my heigh-ho's in her ears:
But if she asks if I for love will die,
Tell her, Good faith, good faith, good faith,—not I.

From ROBERT DOWLAND'S *Musical Banquet*, 1610. (The lines are assigned to ROBERT DEVEREUX, EARL OF ESSEX.)

TO plead my faith, where faith hath no reward,
 To move remorse where favour is not borne,
To heap complaints where she doth not regard,
 Were fruitless, bootless, vain, and yield but scorn.
I loved her whom all the world admired,
 I was refused of her that can love none,
And my vain hopes which far too high aspired
 Is dead and buried and for ever gone.
Forget my name since you have scorned my love,
 And woman-like do not too late lament :
Since for your sake I do all mischief prove,
 I none accuse nor nothing do repent :
I was as fond as ever she was fair,
Yet loved I not more than I now despair.

From *Christ Church MS.* K. 3. 43·5·

SWEET, yet cruel unkind is she
 To creep into my heart and murder me.
Yet those beams from her eyes
Dims Apollo at his rise ;
And all these purer graces,
All in their several places,

Begets a glory doth surprise
All hearts, all eyes,
For only she
Gives life eternity ;
And when her presence deigns but to appear
Never wish greater bliss than shines from her bright
      sphere :
Her absence wounds, strikes dead all hearts with fear.

From CAMPION and ROSSETER'S
Book of Airs, 1601.

WHEN thou must home to shades of underground,
    And there arrived, a new admired guest,
The beauteous spirits do engirt thee round,
White Iope, blithe Helen, and the rest,
To hear the stories of thy finished love
From that smooth tongue whose music hell can move ;

Then wilt thou speak of banqueting delights,
Of masques and revels which sweet youth did make,
Of tourneys and great challenges of knights,
And all these triumphs for thy beauty's sake :
When thou hast told these honours done to thee,
Then tell, O tell, how thou didst murder me.

From ROBERT JONES' *First Book*
of Songs and Airs, 1601.

WHEN love on time and measure makes his
 ground,
 Time that must end, though love can never die,
'Tis love betwixt a shadow and a sound,
 A love not in the heart but in the eye ;
A love that ebbs and flows, now up, now down,
A morning's favour and an evening's frown.

Sweet looks show love, yet they are but as beams :
 Fair words seem true, yet they are but as wind ;
Eyes shed their tears, yet are but outward streams ;
 Sighs paint a shadow in the falsest mind.
Looks, words, tears, sighs show love when love they
 leave ;
False hearts can weep, sigh, swear, and yet deceive.

From FRANCIS PILKINGTON'S
Second Set of Madrigals,
1624.

YOU gentle nymphs that on these meadows play,
 And oft relate the loves of shepherds young,
Come sit you down, for, if you please to stay,
 Now may you hear an uncouth [1] passion sung :
A lad there is, and I am that poor groom,
That's fall'n in love and can not tell with whom.

[1] Strange, unwonted.

From CAMPION and ROSSETER'S
Book of Airs, 1601.

KIND in unkindness, when will you relent
And cease with faint love true love to torment ?
Still entertained, excluded still I stand ;
Her glove still hold, but cannot touch the hand.

In her fair hand my hopes and comforts rest :
O might my fortunes with that hand be blest !
No envious breaths then my deserts could shake,
For they are good whom such true love doth make.

O let not beauty so forget her birth
That it should fruitless home return to earth !
Love is the fruit of beauty, then love one !
Not your sweet self, for such self-love is none.

Love one that only lives in loving you ;
Whose wronged deserts would you with pity view,
This strange distaste which your affection sways
Would relish love, and you find better days.

Thus till my happy sight your beauty views,
Whose sweet remembrance still my hope renews,
Let these poor lines solicit love for me,
And place my joys where my desires would be.

From CAMPION *and* ROSSETER'S
Book of Airs, 1601.

THOUGH you are young and I am old,
    Though your veins hot and my blood cold ;
Though youth is moist and age is dry,
Yet embers live when flames do die.

The tender graft is easily broke,
But who shall shake the sturdy oak ?
You are more fresh and fair than I ;
Yet stubs do live when flowers do die.

Thou, that thy youth doth vainly boast,
Know buds are soonest nipped with frost ;
Think that thy fortune still doth cry,
" Thou fool ! to-morrow thou must die."

From THOMAS WEELKES *Madri-*
gals of Five and Six Parts,
1600.

THREE times a day my prayer is
    To gaze my fill on Thoralis,
And three times thrice I daily pray
Not to offend that sacred may [1] ;
But all the year my suit must be
That I may please and she love me.

[1] Maid.

H

From JOHN DOWLAND'S *Second
Book of Songs or Airs,* 1600.

WHITE as lilies was her face ;
    When she smiled
      She beguiled,
Quitting faith with foul disgrace.
Virtue's service thus neglected
Heart with sorrows hath infected.

When I swore my heart her own,
    She disdained ;
      I complained,
Yet she left me overthrown :
Careless of my bitter grieving,
Ruthless, bent to no relieving.

Vows and oaths and faith assured,
    Constant ever,
      Changing never,—
Yet she could not be procured
To believe my pains exceeding
From her scant respect[1] proceeding.

O that love should have the art,
    By surmises,
      And disguises,
To destroy a faithful heart ;
Or that wanton-looking women
Should reward their friends as foemen.

[1] Old ed. " neglect."

All in vain is ladies' love—
    Quickly choosed,
    Shortly loosed ;
For their pride is to remove.
Out, alas ! their looks first won us,
And their pride hath straight undone us.

To thyself the sweetest Fair !
    Thou hast wounded,
    And confounded
Changeless faith with foul despair ;
And my service hast [1] envied
And my succours hast [1] denied.

By thine error thou hast lost
    Heart unfeigned,
    Truth unstained.
And the swain that loved most,
More assured in love than many,
More despised in love than any.

For my heart, though set at nought,
    Since you will it,
    Spoil and kill it !
I will never change my thought :
But grieve that beauty e'er was born
Thus to answer love with scorn.

[1] Old ed. "hath."

From *Add. MS.* 18936.

PHILLIS, a herd-maid dainty,
    Who hath no peer for beauty,
By Thyrsis was requested
To hear the wrongs wherewith his heart was wrested ;
But she Diana served
And would not hear how Love poor lovers sterved.

Phillis, more white than lilies,
More fair than Amaryllis,
More cold than crystal fountain,
More hard than craggy rock or stony mountain,
O tiger fierce and spiteful,
Why hate'st thou Love sith Love is so delightful?

From ROBERT JONES' *Second Book
of Songs and Airs,* 1601.

MY Love is neither young nor old,
    Not fiery-hot nor frozen-cold,
But fresh and fair as springing-briar
Blooming the fruit of love's desire ;
Not snowy-white nor rosy-red,
But fair enough for shepherd's bed ;
And such a love was never seen
On hill or dale or country-green.

From WILLIAM BYRD'S *Psalms,*
Sonnets, and Songs, 1588.
(Words ascribed to EDWARD
EARL OF OXFORD.)

IF women could be fair and never fond,
   Or that their beauty might continue still,
I would not marvel though they made men bond
   By service long to purchase their goodwill :
But when I see how frail these creatures are,
I laugh that men forget themselves so far.

To mark what choice they make and how they change,
   How, leaving best, the worst they choose out still ;
And how, like haggards wild, about they range,
   And scorning reason follow after will ![1]
Who would not shake such buzzards from the fist
And let them fly (fair fools !) which way they list ?

Yet for our sport we fawn and flatter both,
   To pass the time when nothing else can please :
And train them on to yield by subtle oath
   The sweet content that gives such humour ease :
And then we say, when we their follies try,
" To play with fools, O, what a fool was I !"

---

[1] So Oliphant.—Old ed. " Scorning after reason to follow will.'

From CAMPION and ROSSETER'S
Book of Airs, 1601.

Vivamus, mea Lesbia, atque amemus.

MY sweetest Lesbia, let us live and love,
   And though the sager sort our deeds reprove
Let us not weigh them.   Heaven's great lamps do dive
Into their west, and straight again revive ;
But, soon as once set is our little light,
Then must we sleep one ever-during night.

If all would lead their lives in love like me,
Then bloody swords and armour should not be ;
No drum nor trumpet peaceful sleeps should move,
Unless alarm came from the Camp of Love :
But fools do live and waste their little light,
And seek with pain their ever-during night.

When timely death my life and fortunes ends,
Let not my hearse be vext with mourning friends ;
But let all lovers, rich in triumph, come
And with sweet pastimes grace my happy tomb :
And, Lesbia, close up thou my little light
And crown with love my ever-during night.

From ROBERT JONES' *Second Book
of Songs and Airs,* 1601.

L OVE'S god is a boy,
　　None but cowherds regard him,
His dart is a toy,
Great opinion hath marred him ;
The fear of the wag
Hath made him so brag ;
Chide him, he'll flie thee
And not come nigh thee.
Little boy, pretty knave, shoot not at random,
For if you hit me, slave, I'll tell your grandam.

　　Fond love is a child
　　And his compass is narrow,
　　Young fools are beguiled
　　With the fame of his arrow ;
　　He dareth not strike
　　If his stroke do mislike :
　　Cupid, do you hear me ?
　　Come not too near me.
Little boy, pretty knave, hence I beseech you,
For if you hit me, knave, in faith I'll breech you.

　　Th' ape loves to meddle
　　When he finds a man idle,
　　Else is he a-flirting
　　Where his mark is a-courting ;
　　When women grow true
　　Come teach me to sue,

Then I'll come to thee
Pray thee and woo thee.
Little boy, pretty knave, make me not stagger,
For if you hit me, knave, I'll call thee, beggar.

From THOMAS CAMPION'S *Third
Book of Airs* (circ. 1617).

NOW let her change ! and spare not !
  Since she proves strange, I care not !
Feigned love charmed so my delight,
That still I doted on her sight.
But she is gone ! new joys embracing,
And my distress disgracing.

When did I err in blindness ?
Or vex her with unkindness ?
If my cares served her alone,
Why is she thus untimely gone ?
True love abides to th' hour of dying :
False love is ever flying.

False ! then farewell for ever !
Once false proves faithful never !
He that boasts now of thy love,
Shall soon my present fortunes prove :
Were he as fair as bright Adonis,
Faith is not had where none is.

From ROBERT JONES' *Ultimum
Vale, or Third Book of Airs*
(1608). (Words by "A. W.")

SWEET Love, mine only treasure,
    For service long unfeigned
    Wherein I nought have gained,
Vouchsafe this little pleasure,
    To tell me in what part
    My Lady keeps my [1] heart.

If in her hair so slender,
    Like golden nets entwined
    Which fire and art have 'fined,
Her thrall my heart I render
    For ever to abide
    With locks so dainty tied.

If in her eyes she bind it,
    Wherein that fire was framed
    By which it is enflamed,
I dare not look to find it :
    I only wish it sight
    To see that pleasant light.

But if her breast have deigned
    With kindness to receive it,
    I am content to leave it
Though death thereby were gained.
    Then, Lady, take your own
    That lives by you alone.

[1] So Davison's *Poetical Rhapsody.* The song-book reads "her."

From WILLIAM CORKINE'S *Airs*.
1610.

SOME can flatter, some can feign,
   Simple truth shall plead for me ;
Let not beauty truth disdain,
   Truth is even as fair as she.

But since pairs must equal prove,
   Let my strength her youth oppose,
Love her beauty, faith her love ;
   On even terms so may we close.

Cork or lead in equal weight
   Both one just proportion yield,
So may breadth be peis'd[1] with height,
   Steepest mount with plainest field.

Virtues have not all one kind,
   Yet all virtues merit be,
Divers virtues are combined ;
   Differing so, deserts agree.

Let then love and beauty meet,
   Making one divine concent,[2]
Constant as the sounds and sweet,
   That enchant the firmament.

[1] Balanced.   [2] Harmony.

From CAMPION and ROSSETER'S
Book of Airs, 1601.

S WEET, come again !
     Your happy sight, so much desired
     Since you from hence are now retired,
I seek in vain :
Still I must mourn,
     And pine in longing pain,
     Till you, my life's delight, again
Vouchsafe your wish'd return.

If true desire,
     Or faithful vow of endless love,
     Thy heart inflamed may kindly move
With equal fire ;
O then my joys,
     So long distraught, shall rest,
     Reposed soft in thy chaste breast,
Exempt from all annoys.

You had the power
     My wand'ring thoughts first to restrain,
     You first did hear my love speak plain ;
A child before,
Now is it grown
     Confirmed, do you it keep,
     And let 't safe in your bosom sleep,
There ever made your own !

And till we meet,
    Teach absence inward art to find,
    Both to disturb and please the mind.
Such thoughts are sweet :
And such remain
    In hearts whose flames are true ;
    Then such will I retain, till you
To me return again.

From WILLIAM CORKINE'S Airs,
1610.

SWEET Cupid, ripen her desire,
    Thy joyful harvest may begin ;
If age approach a little nigher,
'Twill be too late to get it in.

Cold winter storms lay standing corn,
Which once too ripe will never rise,
And lovers wish themselves unborn,
When all their joys lie in their eyes.

Then, sweet, let us embrace and kiss :
Shall beauty shale[1] upon the ground?
If age bereave us of this bliss,
Then will no more such sport be found.

1 Shell, husk (as peas).

From RICHARD CARLTON'S *Madrigals*, 1601.

WHEN Flora fair the pleasant tidings bringeth
  Of summer sweet with herbs and flowers
    adorned,
The nightingale upon the hawthorn singeth
And Boreas' blasts the birds and beasts have scorned;
When fresh Aurora with her colours painted,
Mingled with spears of gold, the sun appearing,
Delights the hearts that are with love acquainted,
And maying maids have then their time of cheering;
All creatures then with summer are delighted,
The beasts, the birds, the fish with scale of silver;
Then stately dames by lovers are invited
To walk in meads or row upon the river.
I all alone am from these joys exiled
No summer grows where love yet never smiled.

From GILES FARNABY'S *Canzonets*, 1598.

THRICE blessed be the giver
  That gave sweet love that golden quiver,
And live he long among the gods anointed
That made the arrow-heads sharp-pointed:
If either of them both had quailed,
She of my love and I of hers had failed.

From THOMAS CAMPION'S *Third
Book of Airs* (circ. 1617).

THUS I resolve and Time hath taught me so :
 Since she is fair and ever kind to me,
Though she be wild and wanton-like in show,
 Those little stains in youth I will not see.
That she be constant, heaven I oft implore ;
If prayers prevail not, I can do no more.

Palm-tree the more you press, the more it grows ;
 Leave it alone, it will not much exceed :
Free beauty, if you strive to yoke, you lose,
 And for affection strange distaste you breed.
What nature hath not taught no art can frame ;
Wild-born be wild still, though by force you tame.

From THOMAS WEELKES *Airs or
Fantastic Spirits*, 1608.

THOUGH my carriage be but careless,
 Though my looks be of the sternest,
Yet my passions are compareless ;
 When I love, I love in earnest.

No ; my wits are not so wild,
 But a gentle soul may yoke me ;
Nor my heart so hard compiled,
 But it melts, if love provoke me.

From JOHN DOWLAND'S *Second
Book of Songs or Airs,* 1600.

WOEFUL Heart, with grief oppressed !
　　Since my fortunes most distressed
　From my joys hath me removed,
Follow those sweet eyes adored !
Those sweet eyes wherein are stored
　　All my pleasures best beloved.

Fly my breast—leave me forsaken—
Wherein Grief his seat hath taken,
　　All his arrows through me darting !
Thou mayst live by her sunshining :
I shall suffer no more pining
　　By thy loss than by her parting.

From *Christ Church MS.* 1. 5. 49.

COME, lusty ladies, come, come, come !
　　With pensive thoughts you pine.
Come, learn the galliard now of us,
For we be masquers [fine].
We sing, we dance, and we rejoice
With mirth in modesty :
Come, ladies, then and take a part,
And, as we sing, dance ye !
Tarranta ta-ta-ta-ta-tararantina, &c.

From WILLIAM BYRD'S *Songs of
Sundry Natures,* 1589.

IS Love a boy,—what means he then to strike?
   Or is he blind,—why will he be a guide?
Is he a man,—why doth he hurt his like?
Is he a God,—why doth he men deride?
No one of these, but one compact of all :
A wilful boy, a man still dealing blows,
Of purpose blind to lead men to their thrall,
A god that rules, unruly,—God, he knows.

Boy, pity me that am a child again ;
Blind, be no more my guide to make me stray ;
Man, use thy might to force away my pain ;
God, do me good and lead me to my way ;
And if thou beest a power to me unknown,
Power of my life, let here thy grace be shown.

From THOMAS CAMPION'S *Two
Books of Airs* (circ. 1613).

THE peaceful western wind
　　The winter storms hath tamed,
And Nature in each kind
　The kind heat hath inflamed :
The forward buds so sweetly breathe
　Out of their earthy bowers,
That heaven, which views their pomp beneath,
　Would fain be decked with flowers.

See how the morning smiles
　On her bright eastern hill,
And with soft steps beguiles
　Them that lie slumbering still !
The music-loving birds are come
　From cliffs and rocks unknown,
To see the trees and briars bloom
　That late were overblown.[1]

What Saturn did destroy,
　Love's Queen revives again ;
And now her naked boy
　Doth in the fields remain,
Where he such pleasing change doth view
　In every living thing,
As if the world were born anew
　To gratify the spring.

[1] Old ed. "ouer-flowne."

I

If all things life present,
  Why die my comforts then?
Why suffers my content?
  Am I the worst of men?
O, Beauty, be not thou accused
  Too justly in this case!
Unkindly if true love be used,
  'Twill yield thee little grace.

From JOHN DANYEL'S *Songs for
the Lute, Viol, and Voice,*
1606.

THOU pretty Bird, how do I see
  Thy silly state and mine agree!
For thou a prisoner art;
So is my heart.
Thou sing'st to her, and so do I address
My music to her ear that's merciless;
But herein doth the difference lie,—
That thou art graced, so am not I;
Thou singing livest, and I must singing die.

From THOMAS FORD'S *Music of*
Sundry Kinds, 1607.

WHAT then is Love, sings Corydon,
 Since Phyllida is grown so coy?
A flattering glass to gaze upon,
A busy jest, a serious toy,
A flower still budding, never blown,
A scanty dearth in fullest store,
Yielding least fruit where most is sown.
    My daily note shall be therefore—
    Heigh ho, chill [1] love no more.

'Tis like a morning dewy rose
Spread fairly to the sun's arise,
But when his beams he doth disclose
That which then flourished quickly dies ;
It is a seld-fed dying hope,
A promised bliss, a salveless sore,
An aimless mark, and erring scope.
    My daily note shall be therefore—
    Heigh ho, chill love no more.

'Tis like a lamp shining to all,
Whilst in itself it doth decay ;
It seems to free whom it doth thrall,
And lead[s] our pathless thoughts astray ;
It is the spring of wintered hearts
Parched by the summer's heat before
Faint hope to kindly warmth converts.
    My daily note shall be therefore—
    Heigh ho, chill love no more.

[1] "Chill"—I will.

From MICHAEL ESTE'S *Madri-*
gals of Three, Four, and Five
Parts, 1604.

M Y hope a counsel with my heart
      Hath long desired to be,
And marvels much so dear a friend
   Is not retain'd by me.

She doth condemn my haste
   In passing the estate
Of my whole life into their hands
   Who nought repays but hate :

And not sufficed with this, she says,
   I did release the right
Of my enjoyed liberties
   Unto your beauteous sight.

From John Wilbye's *Madrigals,*
1598.

SWEET Love, if thou wilt gain a monarch's glory,
Subdue her heart who makes me glad and sorry;
Out of thy golden quiver,
Take thou thy strongest arrow
That will through bone and marrow,
And me and thee of grief and fear deliver :
But come behind, for, if she look upon thee,
Alas ! poor Love, then thou art woe-begone thee.

From Thomas Weelkes' *Ballets
and Madrigals,* 1598.

SWEET Love, I will no more abuse thee,
Nor with my voice accuse thee ;
But tune my notes unto thy praise
And tell the world Love ne'er decays.
Sweet Love doth concord ever cherish :
What wanteth concord soon must perish.

From ROBERT JONES' *Ultimum
Vale or Third Book of Airs*
(1608).

THINK'ST thou, Kate, to put me down
  With a ' No ' or with a frown?
Since Love holds my heart in bands
I must do as Love commands.

Love commands the hands to dare
When the tongue of speech is spare
Chiefest lesson in Love's school,—
Put it in adventure, fool !

Fools are they that fainting flinch
For a squeak, a scratch, a pinch :
Women's words have double sense :
' Stand away ! '—a simple fence.

If thy mistress swear she'll cry,
Fear her not, she'll swear and lie :
Such sweet oaths no sorrow bring
Till the prick of conscience sting.

From ROBERT JONES' *First Book
of Airs,* 1601.

A WOMAN'S looks
   Are barbed hooks,
  That catch by art
  The strongest heart
When yet they spend no breath ;
   But let them speak,
   And sighing break
  Forth into tears,
  Their words are spears
That wound our souls to death.

   The rarèst wit
   Is made forget,
  And like a child
  Is oft beguiled
With love's sweet-seeming bait ;
   Love with his rod
   So like a God
  Commands the mind ;
  We cannot find,
Fair shows hide foul deceit.

   Time, that all things
   In order brings,
  Hath taught me how
  To be more slow
In giving faith to speech,

Since women's words
No truth affords,
And when they kiss
They think by this
Us men to over-reach.

From JOHN DOWLAND's *Third
and last Book of Songs and
Airs*, 1603. (Words ascribed
to SIR EDWARD DYER.)

THE lowest trees have tops, the ant her gall,
   The fly her spleen, the little spark his heat;
And slender hairs cast shadows, though but small,
   And bees have stings, although they be not great;
Seas have their source, and so have shallow springs;
And love is love in beggars and in kings!

Where waters smoothest run, deep are the fords;
   The dial stirs, yet none perceives it move;
The firmest faith is in the fewest words;
   The turtles cannot sing, and yet they love;
True hearts have eyes and ears, no tongues to speak;
They hear, and see, and sigh, and then they break!

From MICHAEL ESTE'S *Madrigals of Three, Four, and Five Parts,* 1604. (By NICHOLAS BRETON. Originally published in 1591.)

IN the merry month of May,
  On a morn by break of day,
Forth I walk'd by the wood-side,
Whereas May was in her pride :
There I spyed all alone
Phillida and Corydon.
Much ado there was, God wot !
He would love and she would not.
She said, never man was true ;
He said, none was false to you.
He said, he had loved her long ;
She said, Love should have no wrong.
Corydon would kiss her then ;
She said, maids must kiss no men
Till they did for good and all ;
Then she made the shepherd call
All the heavens to witness truth
Never loved a truer youth.
Thus with many a pretty oath,
Yea and nay, and faith and troth,
Such as seely shepherds use
When they will not love abuse,
Love, which had been long deluded,
Was with kisses sweet concluded ;
And Phillida with garlands gay
Was made the Lady of the May.

From ROBERT JONES' *First Book*
of Airs, 1601.

O MY poor eyes, the sun whose shine
    Late gave you light, doth now decline
And, set to you, to others riseth.
She, who would sooner die than change,
Not fearing death, delights to range,
        And now, O now, my soul despiseth.

Yet, O my heart, thy state is blest
To seek out rest in thy unrest,
        Since thou her slave no more remainest ;
For she that bound thee sets thee free
Then when she first forsaketh thee :
        Such, O such, right by wrong thou gainest.

Eyes, gaze no more ! heart, learn to hate !
Experience tells you, all too late,
        Fond woman's love with faith still warreth :
While true desert speaks, writes and gives,
Some groom the bargain nearer drives
        And he, O he, the market marreth.

From CAMPION and ROSSETER'S
Book of Airs, 1601.

SEE where she flies enraged from me !
  View her when she intends despite,
The wind is not more swift than she.
Her fury moved such terror makes
As to a fearful guilty sprite
The voice of heaven's huge thunder-cracks :
But when her appeased mind yields to delight,
All her thoughts are made of joys,
Millions of delights inventing ;
Other pleasures are but toys
To her beauty's sweet contenting.

My fortune hangs upon her brow ;
For as she smiles or frowns on me,
So must my blown affections bow ;
And her proud thoughts too well do find
With what unequal tyranny
Her beauties do command my mind.
Though, when her sad planet reigns,
Froward she be,
She alone can pleasure move
And displeasing sorrow banish.
May I but still hold her love,
Let all other comforts vanish.

From FRANCIS PILKINGTON'S
First Set of Madrigals, 1614.

SEE where my love a-maying goes,
   With sweet dame Flora sporting !
She most alone with nightingales
   In woods delights consorting.
Turn again, my dearest !
   The pleasant'st air's in meadows :
Else by the rivers let us breathe,
   And kiss amongst the willows.

From WILLIAM CORKINE'S
Second Book of Airs, 1612.

SHALL a smile or guileful glance,
   Or a sigh that is but feigned,
Shall but tears that come by chance
   Make me dote that was disdained ?
   No ; I will no more be chained.

Shall I sell my freedom so,
   Being now from Love remised ?
Shall I learn (what I do know
   To my cost) that Love's disguised ?
   No ; I will be more advised.

Must she fall, and I must stand ?
   Must she fly, and I pursue her ?
Must I give her heart and land,
   And, for nought, with them endue her ?
   No ; first I will find her truer.

From WILLIAM CORKINE'S *Airs*,
1610.

SHALL a frown or angry eye,
   Shall a word unfitly placed,
Shall a shadow make me flie
    As if I were with tigers chased?
    Love must not be so disgraced.

Shall I woo her in despight?
   Shall I turn her from her flying?
Shall I tempt her with delight?
    Shall I laugh at her denying?
    No : beware of lovers' crying.

Shall I then with patient mind,
   Still attend her wayward pleasure?
Time will make her prove more kind,
    Let her coyness then take leisure :
    She is worthy such a treasure.

From RICHARD ALISON'S *An
Hour's Recreation in Music*,
1606.

SHALL I abide this jesting?
   I weep, and she's a-feasting !
O cruel fancy, that so doth blind me
To love one that doth not mind me !

Can I abide this prancing?
I weep, and she's a-dancing !
O cruel fancy, so to betray me !
Thou goest about to slay me.

From ROBERT JONES *Ultimum
Vale*, 1608. (Words by
FRANCIS DAVISON.)

SWEET, if you like and love me still
    And yield me love for my good will,
And do not from your promise start
When your fair hand gave me your heart ;
    If dear to you I be
    As you are dear to me,
Then yours I am and will be ever :
Nor[1] time nor place my love shall sever,
But faithful still I will persèver,
        Like constant marble stone,
        Loving but you alone.

But if you favour moe[2] than me
(Who loves thee still and none but thee),
If others do the harvest gain
That's due to me for all my pain ;
    If[3] that you love to range
    And oft to chop and change,
Then get you some new-fangled mate ;
My doting love shall turn to hate,
Esteeming you (though too-too late)
        Not worth a pebble stone,
        Loving not me alone.[4]

[1] This is the reading in Davison's *Poetical Rhapsody*, where
this song is printed with the heading "His farewell to his unkind
and inconstant mistress."—The song-book gives "No time nor
place."

[2] "Moe"—old form of "more."

[3] Old ed. "Yet."

[4] So Davison.—In the song-book the line stands "Loving
me not alone."

From JOHN DOWLAND'S *Third
Book of Songs or Airs*, 1603.

' SAY, Love, if ever thou didst find
        A woman with a constant mind.'
                    ' None but one.'
' And what should that rare mirror be ? '
' Some goddess or some queen is She.'
She, She, She, and only She,
She only queen of love and beauty.

' But could thy fiery poisoned dart
At no time touch her spotless heart,
                    Nor come near ? '
' She is not subject to Love's bow :
Her eye commands, her heart saith " No."
No, no, no, and only No,
One No another still doth follow.

' How might I that fair wonder know
That mocks desire with endless " No ? " '
                    ' See the moon
That ever in one change doth grow,
Yet still the same : and She is so.'
So, so, so, and only So !
From heaven her virtues she doth borrow.

' To her then yield thy shafts and bow
That can command affections so.'
                    ' Love is free :

So are her thoughts that vanquish thee.
There is no queen of love but She.'
She, She, She, and only She,
She only queen of love and beauty.

From THOMAS WEELKES' *Ballets
and Madrigals*, 1598.

FAREWELL, my joy !
     Adieu my love and pleasure !
To sport and toy
     We have no longer leisure.
          Fa la la !

Farewell, adieu
     Until our next consorting !
Sweet love, be true !
     And thus we end our sporting.
          Fa la la !

From JOHN WILBYE's *Second Set of Madrigals*, 1609.

COME, shepherd swains, that wont to hear me sing,
    Now sigh and groan !
Dead is my Love, my Hope, my Joy, my Spring ;
    Dead, dead, and gone !
O, She that was your Summer's Queen,
    Your days' delight,
Is gone and will no more be seen ;
    O, cruel spite !
Break all your pipes that wont to sound
    With pleasant cheer,
And cast yourselves upon the ground
    To wail my Dear !
Come, shepherd swains, come, nymphs, and all a-row
    To help me cry :
Dead is my Love, and, seeing She is so,
    Lo, now I die !

K

From DR. JOHN WILSON'S *Cheer-*
ful Airs or Ballads, 1660.
(Words by SIR ALBERTUS
MORTON.)

GREEDY lover, pause awhile,
  And remember that a smile
      Heretofore
Would have made thy hopes a feast ;
      Which is more,
Since thy diet was increased,
Than both looks and language too,
Or the face itself, can do.

Such a province was my hand
As, if it thou couldst command
      Heretofore,
There thy lips would seem to dwell ;
      Which is more,
Ever since they sped so well,
Than they can be brought to do
By my neck and bosom too.

If the centre of my breast,
A dominion unpossest
      Heretofore,
May thy wandering thoughts suffice,
      Seek no more,
And my heart shall be thy prize :
So thou keep above the line,
All the hemisphere is thine.

If the flames of love were pure,
Which by oath thou didst assure
     Heretofore,
Gold that goes into the clear
     Shines the more
When it leaves again the fire :
Let not then those looks of thine
Blemish what they should refine.

I have cast into the fire
Almost all thou couldst desire
     Heretofore ;
But I see thou art to crave
     More and more.
Should I cast in all I have,
So that I were ne'er so free,
Thou wouldst burn, though not for me.

From JOHN FARMER'S *First Set of*
English Madrigals, 1599.

A LITTLE pretty bonny lass was walking
  In midst of May before the sun gan rise ;
I took her by the hand and fell to talking
  Of this and that as best I could devise :
I swore I would—yet still she said I should not ;
Do what I would, and yet for all I could not.

From ROBERT JONES' *Ultimum*
Vale, 1608.

CEASE, troubled thoughts, to sigh or sigh yourselves
          to death,
Or kindle not my grief or cool it with your breath :
     Let not that spirit which made me live
     Seek thus untimely to deprive
          Me of my life :
          Unequal strife,
That breath which gave me being
Should hasten me to dying !

Cease, melting tears, to stream, stop your uncessant
          course,
Which to my sorrow's child are like a fruitful nurse,
     From whence death living comfort draws ;
     And I myself appear the cause
          Of all my woe ;
          But 'tis not so,
For she, whose beauty won me,
By falsehood hath undone me.

From THOMAS BATESON s *Second
Set of Madrigals,* 1618.

CUPID, in a bed of roses
    Sleeping, chanced to be stung
    Of a bee that lay among
The flowers where he himself reposes ;
And thus to his mother weeping
    Told that he this wound did take
    Of a little winged snake,
As he lay securely sleeping.
Cytherea smiling said
    That " if so great sorrow spring
    From a silly bee's weak sting
As should make thee thus dismay'd,
What anguish feel they, think'st thou, and what pain,
Whom thy empoison'd arrows cause complain ? "

From WILLIAM CORKINE'S *Airs,*
1610.

SWEET, let me go ! sweet, let me go !
    What do you mean to vex me so ?
Cease your pleading force !
Do you think thus to extort remorse ?
Now, now ! no more ! alas, you overbear me,
And I would cry,—but some would hear, I fear me.

From THOMAS GREAVES' *Songs
of Sundry Kinds,* 1604.

LADY, the melting crystal of your eye
　　Like frozen drops upon your cheeks did lie ;
Mine eye was dancing on them with delight,
And saw love's flames within them burning bright,
Which did mine eye entice
To play with burning ice ;
But O, my heart thus sporting with desire,
My careless eye did set my heart on fire.

O that a drop from such a sweet fount flying
Should flame like fire and leave my heart a-dying !
I burn, my tears can never drench it
Till in your eyes I bathe my heart and quench it :
But there, alas, love with his fire lies sleeping,
And all conspire to burn my heart with weeping.

From THOMAS WEELKES'*Madrigals of Five and Six Parts,*
1600.

NOW let us make a merry greeting
　　And thank God Cupid for our meeting :
My heart is full of joy and pleasure
Since thou art here, mine only treasure.
Now will we dance and sport and play
And sing a merry roundelay.

From THOMAS CAMPION'S *Two
Books of Airs* (circ. 1613).

THERE is none, O none but you,
 That from me estrange your sight,
Whom mine eyes affect to view
 Or chained ears hear with delight.

Other beauties others move,
 In you I all graces find ;
Such is the effect of Love,
 To make them happy that are kind.

Women in frail beauty trust,
 Only seem you fair to me ;
Yet prove truly kind and just,
 For that may not dissembled be.

Sweet, afford me then your sight,
 That, surveying all your looks,
Endless volumes I may write
 And fill the world with envied books :

Which when after-ages view,
 All shall wonder and despair,
Woman to find man so true,
 Or man a woman half so fair.

From ROBERT JONES' *First Book*
of Songs and Airs, 1601.

WOMEN, what are they? Changing weather-
        cocks
That smallest puffs of lust have power to turn.
Women, what are they? Virtue's stumbling-blocks
Whereat weak fools do fall, the wiser spurn.
We men, what are we? Fools and idle boys
To spend our time in sporting with such toys.

Women, what are they? Trees whose outward rind
Makes show for fair when inward heart is hollow.
Women, what are they? Beasts of hyena's kind
That speak those fair'st whom most they mean to
        swallow.
We men, what are we? fools and idle boys
To spend our time in sporting with such toys.

Women, what are they? rocks upon the coast
Whereon we suffer shipwrack at our landing.
Women, what are they? patient creatures most
That rather yield than strive 'gainst aught with-
        standing.
We men, what are we? Fools and idle boys
To spend our time in sporting with such toys.

From THOMAS CAMPION'S *Third
Book of Airs* (circ. 1617).

SO quick, so hot, so mad is thy fond suit,
  So rude, so tedious grown in urging me,
That fain I would with loss make thy tongue mute,
  And yield some little grace to quiet thee :
An hour with thee I care not to converse,
For I would not be counted too perverse.

But roofs too hot would prove for me[1] all fire,
  And hills too high for my unused pace ;
The grove is charged with thorns and the bold briar,
  Grey snakes the meadows shroud in every place :
A yellow frog, alas ! will fright me so
As I should start and tremble as I go.

Since then I can on earth no fit room find,
  In heaven I am resolved with you to meet :
Till then, for hope's sweet sake, rest your tired mind,
  And not so much as see me in the street :
A heavenly meeting one day we shall have,
But never, as you dream, in bed or grave.

[1] Old ed. " men."

From THOMAS MORLEY'S *First
Book of Ballets to Five Voices*,
1595.

SHOOT, false Love! I care not ;
    Spend thy shafts and spare not !
                    Fa la la !
I fear not, I, thy might,
And less I weigh thy spite ;
All naked I unarm me,—
If thou can'st, now shoot and harm me !
So lightly I esteem thee
As now a child I deem thee.
                    Fa la la !

Long thy bow did fear[1] me,
While thy pomp did blear me ;
                    Fa la la !
But now I do perceive
Thy art is to deceive ;
And every simple lover
All thy falsehood can discover.
Then weep, Love ! and be sorry,
For thou hast lost thy glory.
                    Fa la la !

Frighten.

From JOHN DOWLAND'S *First
Book of Songs or Airs*, 1597.

DEAR, if you change, I'll never choose again ;
  Sweet, if you shrink, I'll never think of love ;
Fair, if you fail, I'll judge all beauty vain ;
Wise, if too weak, more wits I'll never prove.
Dear, sweet, fair, wise ! change, shrink, nor be not
      weak ;
And, on my faith, my faith shall never break.

Earth with her flowers shall sooner heaven adorn ;
Heaven her bright stars through earth's dim globe
      shall move ;
Fire heat shall lose, and frosts of flames be born ;
Air, made to shine, as black as hell shall prove :
Earth, heaven, fire, air, the world transformed shall
      view,
Ere I prove false to faith or strange to you.

From THOMAS CAMPION'S *Third
Book of Airs* (circ. 1617).

KIND are her answers,
  But her performance keeps no day
Breaks time, as dancers,
From their own music when they stray.
All her free favours and smooth words
Wing my hopes in vain.
O, did ever voice so sweet but only feign?
Can true love yield such delay,
Converting joy to pain?

Lost is our freedom
When we submit to women so:
Why do we need 'em
When, in their best, they work our woe?
There is no wisdom
Can alter ends by Fate prefixt.
O, why is the good of man with evil mixt?
Never were days yet called two
But one night went betwixt.

From MICHAEL ESTE'S *Madri-*
gals, 1604.

SLY thief, if so you will believe,
   It nought or little did me grieve,
That my true heart you had bereft,
Till that unkindly you it left :
Leaving you lose, losing you kill
That which I may forego so ill.

What thing more cruel can you do
Than rob a man and kill him too?
Wherefore of love I ask this meed,
To bring you where you did this deed,
That there you may, for your amisses[1]
Be damaged in a thousand kisses.

[1] Faults.

From THOMAS CAMPION'S *Two
Books of Airs* (circ. 1613).

HOW eas'ly wert thou chained,
　 Fond heart, by favours feigned !
Why lived thy hopes in grace,
Straight to die disdained ?
But since thou'rt now beguiled
By love that falsely smiled,
In some less happy place
Mourn alone exiled.
My love still here increaseth,
And with my love my grief,
While her sweet bounty ceaseth,
That gave my woes relief.
Yet 'tis no woman leaves me,
For such may prove unjust ;
A goddess thus deceives me !
Whose faith who could mistrust ?

A goddess so much graced
That Paradise is placed
In her most heav'nly breast,
Once by Love embraced.
But Love, that so kind proved,
Is now from her removed ;
Nor will he longer rest
Where no faith is loved.

If powers celestial wound us
And will not yield relief,
Woe then must needs confound us,
For none can cure our grief.
No wonder if I languish
Through burden of my smart :
It is no common anguish
From Paradise to part.

From THOMAS CAMPION'S *Fourth
Book of Airs* (circ. 1617).

SO sweet is thy discourse to me,
    And so delightful is thy sight,
As I taste nothing right but thee :
    O why invented Nature light ?
Was it alone for Beauty's sake
That her graced words might better take ?

No more can I old joys recall,
    They now to me become unknown,
Not seeming to have been at all :
    Alas, how soon is this love grown
To such a spreading height in me
As with it all must shadowed be !

From WILLIAM BYRD'S *Psalms,
Sonnets, and Songs,* 1588.

FAREWELL, false Love, the oracle of lies,
    A mortal foe and enemy to rest,
An envious boy from whom all cares arise,
    A bastard vile, a beast with rage possest ;
A way of error, a temple full of treason,
In all effects contrary unto reason.

A poison'd serpent cover'd all with flowers,
    Mother of sighs and murderer of repose ;
A sea of sorrows from whence are drawn such showers
    As moisture lend to every grief that grows ;
A school of guile, a net of deep deceit,
A gilded hook that holds a poison'd bait.

A fortress foiled which Reason did defend,
    A Siren song, a fever of the mind,
A maze wherein affection finds no end,
    A raging cloud that runs before the wind ;
A substance like the shadow of the sun,
A goal of grief for which the wisest run.

A quenchless fire, a nurse of trembling fear,
    A path that leads to peril and mishap,
A true retreat of sorrow and despair,
    An idle boy that sleeps in Pleasure's lap ;
A deep distrust of that which certain seems,
A hope of that which Reason doubtful deems.

From JOHN DOWLAND'S *First
Book of Songs or Airs*, 1597.

REST awhile, you cruel cares,
    Be not more severe than love ;
Beauty kills and beauty spares,
And sweet smiles sad sighs remove.
Laura, fair queen of my delight,
Come, grant me love in love's despite ;
And if I ever fail to honour thee,
        Let this heavenly light I see
        Be as dark as hell to me !

If I speak, my words want weight ;
Am I mute, my heart doth break ;
If I sigh, she fears deceit ;
Sorrow then for me must speak.
Cruel, unkind, with favour view
The wound that first was made by you !
And if my torments feigned be,
        Let this heavenly light I see
        Be as dark as hell to me !

Never hour of pleasing rest
Shall revive my dying ghost
Till my soul hath repossest
The sweet hope which love hath lost.
Laura, reedem the soul that dies
By fury of thy murdering eyes ;
And if it proves unkind to thee,
        Let this heavenly light I see
        Be as dark as hell to me !

L.

From John Dowland's *First
Book of Songs or Airs,* 1597.

UNQUIET thoughts, your civil slaughter stint,
  And wrap your wrongs within a pensive heart ;
And you, my tongue, that makes my mouth a mint
And stamps my thoughts to coin them words by art,
Be still ! for if you ever do the like,
I'll cut the string that makes the hammer strike.

But what can stay my thoughts they may not start?
Or put my tongue in durance for to die?
Whenas these eyes, the keys of mouth and heart,
Open the lock where all my love doth lie,
I'll seal them up within their lids for ever :
So thoughts and words and looks shall die together.

How shall I then gaze on my mistress' eyes?
My thoughts must have some vent, else heart will
      break.
My tongue would rust, as in my mouth it lies,
If eyes and thoughts were free and that not speak.
Speak then ! and tell the passions of desire,
Which turns mine eyes to floods, my thoughts to fire.

From JOHN BARTLET's *Airs,*
1606.

WHEN from my love I looked for love and kind
affection's due,
Too well I found her vows to prove most faithless and
untrue ;
For when I did ask her why,
Most sharply she did reply
That she with me did ne'er agree
To love but jestingly.

Mark the subtle policies that female lovers find,
Who loves to fix their constancies like feathers in the
wind ;
Though they swear, vow, and protest
That they love you chiefly best,
Yet by-and-by they'll all deny,
And say 'twas but in jest.

From THOMAS WEELKES' *Madrigals,* 1597.

YOUNG Cupid hath proclaimed a bloody war
And vows revenge on all the maiden crew :
Oh yield, fair Chloris, lest in that foul jar
Thine after penance makes thy folly rue.
And yet I fear, her wondrous beauty's such,
A thousand Cupids dare not Chloris touch.

From THOMAS BATESON'S *First
Set of English Madrigals,*
1604.

M USIC, some think, no music is
    Unless she sing of clip and kiss
And bring to wanton tunes " Fie, fie !"
Or " Tih-ha tah-ha !" or " I'll cry !"
But let such rhymes no more disgrace
Music sprung of heavenly race.

From ROBERT JONES *A Musical
Dream,* 1609.

M Y complaining is but feigning,
    All my love is but in jest ;
                        (Fa, la, la !)
And my courting is but sporting,
    In most shewing meaning least.
                        (Fa, la, la !)
Outward sadness inward gladness
    Representeth in my mind ;
                        (Fa, la, la !)
In most feigning most obtaining,
    Such good faith in love I find.
                        (Fa, la, la !)
Towards ladies this my trade is,
    Two minds in one breast I wear ;
                        (Fa, la, la !)
And, my measure at my pleasure,
    Ice and flame my face doth bear.
                        (Fa, la, la !)

From THOMAS CAMPION'S *Fourth
Book of Airs* (circ. 1617).

THOU joy'st, fond boy, to be by many loved,
   To have thy beauty of most dames approved ;
For this dost thou thy native worth disguise
And play'st the sycophant t'observe their eyes :
Thy glass thou counsell'st, more to adorn thy skin,
That first should school thee to be fair within.

'Tis childish to be caught with pearl or amber,
And womanlike too much to cloy the chamber ;
Youths should the fields affect, heat their rough steeds,
Their hardened nerves to fit for better deeds :
Is't not more joy strongholds to force with swords
Than women's weakness take with looks or words ?

Men that do noble things all purchase glory,
One man for one brave act hath proved a story ;
But if that one ten thousand dames o'ercame,
Who would record it, if not to his shame ?
'Tis far more conquest with one to live true
Than every hour to triumph lord of new.

From CAMPION and ROSSETER'S
Book of Airs, 1601.

TURN back, you wanton flyer,
  And answer my desire
With mutual greeting.
Yet bend a little nearer,
True beauty still shines clearer
  In closer meeting.
Hearts with hearts delighted
Should strive to be united,
  Each other's arms with arms enchaining :
Hearts with a thought,
  Rosy lips with a kiss still entertaining.

What harvest half so sweet is
As still to reap the kisses
  Grown ripe in sowing?
And straight to be receiver
Of that which thou art giver,
  Rich in bestowing ?
There's no strict observing
Of times' or seasons' swerving,[1]
  There is ever one fresh spring abiding :
Then what we sow with our lips,
  Let us reap, love's gains dividing.

[1] Old ed. "changing."

From ROBERT JONES' *First Book
of Songs and Airs,* 1601.

WHERE lingering fear doth once possess the
    heart,
    There is the tongue
    Forced to prolong
And smother up his suit, while that his smart,
Like fire supprest, flames more in every part.

Who dares not speak deserves not his desire ;
    The boldest face
    Findeth most grace ;
Though women love that men should them admire,
They slily laugh at him dares come no higher.

Some think a glance, expressed by a sigh,
    Winning the field,
    Maketh them yield :
But while these glancing fools do roll the eye,
They beat the bush, away the bird doth flie.

A gentle heart in vertuous breast doth stay ;
    Pity doth dwell
    In Beauty's cell ;
A woman's heart doth not, though tongue, say " Nay : "
Repentance taught me this the other day.

Which had I wist, I presently had got
    The pleasing fruit
    Of my long suit ;
But Time hath now beguiled me of this lot,
For that by his foretop I took him not.

From THOMAS CAMPION'S *Fourth Book of Airs* (circ. 1617).

BEAUTY is but a painted hell :
　　Ay me, ay me !
She wounds them that admire it,
She kills them that desire it.
　　Give her pride but fuel,
　　No fire is more cruel.

Pity from every heart is fled :
　　Ay me, ay me !
Since false desire could borrow
Tears of dissembled sorrow,
　　Constant vows turn truthless,
　　Love cruel, Beauty ruthless.

Sorrow can laugh and Fury sing :
　　Ay, me, ay me !
My raving griefs discover
I lived too true a lover.
　　The first step to madness
　　Is excess of sadness.

From JOHN MUNDY'S *Songs and Psalms*, 1594.

HEIGH ho! chill[1] go to plough no more!
    Sit down and take thy rest;
Of golden groats I have full store
    To flaunt it with the best.
But I love and I love, and who thinks you?
The finest lass that e'er you knew:
Which makes me sing when I should cry
Heigh ho! for love I die.

From ROBERT JONES' *First Book of Songs and Airs*, 1601.

FAREWELL, dear love! since thou wilt needs be
    gone:
Mine eyes do show my life is almost done.
      —Nay I will never die,
      So long as I can spy;
      There be many mo
      Though that she do go.
There be many mo, I fear not;
Why, then, let her go, I care not.—

Farewell, farewell! since this I find is true,
I will not spend more time in wooing you.
      —But I will seek elsewhere
      If I may find her there.
      Shall I bid her go?
      What and if I do?
Shall I bid her go and spare not?
O no, no, no, no, I dare not.—

        1 "Chill"—I will

Ten thousand times farewell ! yet stay awhile.
Sweet, kiss me once, sweet kisses time beguile.
  —I have no power to move :
  How now, am I in love !—
  Wilt thou needs be gone ?
  Go then, all is one.
Wilt thou needs be gone ?   O hie thee !
Nay ; stay, and do no more deny me.

Once more farewell ! I see *Loth to depart.*[1]
Bids oft adieu to her that holds my heart :
  But seeing I must lose
  Thy love which I did choose,
  Go thy ways for me,
  Since it may not be :
Go thy ways for me, but whither
Go,—oh but where I may come thither.

What shall I do ? my love is now departed,
She is as fair as she is cruel-hearted :
  She would not be entreated
  With prayers oft repeated.
  If she come no more,
  Shall I die therefore ?
If she come no more, what care I ?
—Faith, let her go, or come, or tarry !

 1 There was an old song with this title.—See Chappell's *Popu
lar Music of the Olden Time,* p. 173.

From GILES FARNABY'S *Canzonets,* 1598.

SOMETIME she would and sometime nct,
 The more request the more disdained;
Each woman hath her gift, God wot,
 And ever had since Venus reigned:
Though Vulcan did to Venus yield,
I would have men to win the field.

From JOHN WILBYE's *Second Set
of Madrigals,* 1609.

STAY, Corydon, thou swain,
 Talk not so soon of dying;
What, though thy heart be slain,
 What, if thy love be flying?
She threatens thee, but dare not strike;
 Thy nymph is light and shadow-like,
For if thou follow her she'll fly from thee,
But if thou fly from her she'll follow thee.

From THOMAS MORLEY'S *Ma-*
drigals to Four Voices, 1600.

ON a fair morning, as I came by the way,
    Met I with a merry maid in the merry month of
        May,
When a sweet love sings his lovely lay
And every bird upon the bush bechirps it up so gay,
With a heave and ho ! with a heave and ho !
Thy wife shall be thy master, I trow.
Sing, care away, care away, let the world go !
Hey, lustily all in a row, all in a row,
Sing, care away, care away, let the world go !

From DR. JOHN WILSON'S *Cheer-*
ful Airs or Ballads, 1660.
(Words by ROBERT HEATH.)

YOU say you love me, nay, can swear it too ;
    But stay, sir, 'twill not do.
I know you keep your oaths
Just as you wear your clothes,
While new and fresh in fashion ;
But once grown old,
You lay them by,
Forgot like words you speak in passion.
I'll not believe you, I.

From CAMPION AND ROSSETER'S
Book of Airs, 1601.

WHEN the god of merry love
As yet in his cradle lay,
Thus his withered nurse did say :
" Thou a wanton boy wilt prove
To deceive the powers above ;
For by thy continual smiling
I see thy power of beguiling."

Therewith she the babe did kiss ;
When a sudden fire outcame
From those burning lips of his
That did her with love inflame,
But none would regard the same :
So that, to her day of dying,
The old wretch lived ever crying.

From CAMPION and ROSSETER'S
Book of Airs, 1601.

WHEN to her lute Corinna sings,
Her voice revives the leaden strings,
And doth in highest notes appear
As any challenged echo clear ;
But when she doth of mourning speak,
E'en with her sighs the strings do break.

And as her lute doth live or die,
Led by her passion, so must I :
For when of pleasure she doth sing,
My thoughts enjoy a sudden spring;
But if she doth of sorrow speak,
E'en from my heart the strings do break.

From ROBERT JONES' *Ultimum
Vale,* 1608.

WHEN will the fountain of my tears be dry,
   When will my sighs be spent?
When will desire agree to let me die?
   When will thy heart relent?
It is not for my life I plead,
Since death the way to rest doth lead ;
         But stay for thy consent,
         Lest thou be discontent.

For if myself without thy leave I kill,
   My ghost will never rest ;
So hath it sworn to work thine only will
   And holds it ever best ;
For since it only lives by thee,
Good reason thou the ruler be :
         Then give me leave to die,
         And show thy power thereby.

DROWN not with tears, my dearest Love,
  Those eyes which my affections move ;
  Do not with weeping those lights blind
  Which me in thy subjection bind.
  Time, that made us two of one,
  And forced thee now to live alone,
  Will once again us re-unite
  To show how she can Fortune spite.
  Then will we our time redeem,
  And hold our hours in more esteem,
  Turning all our sweetest nights
  Into millions of delights ;
  And strive with many thousand kisses
  To multiply exchange of blisses.

FAIR Hebe, when dame Flora meets,
    She trips and leaps as gallants do ;
  Up to the hills and down again
    To the vallies runs she to and fro.
  But out, alas ! when frosty locks
    Begirds the head with cark and care,
  Peace ! laugh no more, let pranks go by,
    Slow-crawling age forbids such ware.

From ORLANDO GIBBONS' *First
Set of Madrigals*, 1612.

FAIR is the rose, yet fades with heat or cold ;
    Sweet are the violets, yet soon grown old ;
The lily 's white, yet in one day 'tis done ;
White is the snow, yet melts against the sun :
So white, so sweet, was my fair mistress' face,
Yet altered quite in one short hour's [1] space :
So short-lived beauty a vain gloss doth borrow,
Breathing delight to-day, but none to-morrow.

From THOMAS MORLEY S *First
Book of Ballets to Five Voices*,
1595.

THUS saith my Galatea :
    Love long hath been deluded,
When shall it be concluded?

The young nymphs all are wedded :
    Ah, then why do I tarry?
    Oh, let me die or marry.

---

[1] " Hour " is here (as frequently in the Elizabethan poets) to
be pronounced as a dissyllable.   In fact it was commonly spelt
" hower."

From JOHN ATTYE'S *First Book
of Airs,* 1622.

ON a time the amorous Silvy
  Said to her shepherd, 'Sweet, how do you?
Kiss me this once, and then God be wi' you,
                        My sweetest dear !
Kiss me this once and then God be wi' you,
For now the morning draweth near.'

With that, her fairest bosom showing,
Opening her lips, rich perfumes blowing,
She said, 'Now kiss me and be going,
                        My sweetest dear !
Kiss me this once and then be going,
For now the morning draweth near.'

With that the shepherd waked from sleeping,
And, spying where the day was peeping,
He said, 'Now take my soul in keeping,
                        My sweetest dear !
Kiss me, and take my soul in keeping,
Since I must go, now day is near.'

M

From ORLANDO GIBBONS' *First
Set of Madrigals,* 1612.

L AIS, now old, that erst all-tempting [1] lass,
   To Goddess Venus consecrates her glass ;
For she herself hath now no use of one,
No dimpled cheeks hath she to gaze upon :
She cannot see her springtide damask grace,
Nor dare she look upon her winter face.

From JOHN DANYEL'S *Songs for
the Lute, Viol, and Voice,*
1606.

W HAT delight can they enjoy
      Whose hearts are not their own,
But are gone abroad astray
   And to others' bosoms flown ?
Silly comforts, silly joy,
   Which fall and rise as others move
Who seldom use to turn our way !
   And therefore Chloris will not love,
         For well I see
         How false men be,
   And let them pine that lovers prove.

[1] Old ed. "attempting."

From ROBERT JONES' *First Book of Airs*, 1601.

WHAT if I seek for love of thee ?
　　Shall I find
　　Beauty kind,
To desert that still shall dwell in me ?
Though thy looks have charmed mine eyes,
I can forbear to love ;
　　But if ever sweet desire
　　Set my woeful heart on fire,
Then can I never remove.

Frown not on me unless thou hate ;
　　For thy frown
　　Cast[s] me down
To despair of my most hapless state.
Smile not on me unless thou love ;
　　For thy smile
　　Will beguile
My desires, if thou unsteadfast prove.
If thou needs wilt bend thy brows,
A-while refrain, my dear ;
　　But if thou wilt smile on me,
　　Let it not delayed be :
Comfort is never too near.

From THOMAS FORD'S *Music of
Sundry Kinds,* 1607.

UNTO the temple of thy Beauty,
    And to the tomb where Pity lies,
I, pilgrim-clad with zeal and duty,
    Do offer up my heart, mine eyes.
My heart, lo ! in the quenchless fire,
    On Love's burning altar lies,
Conducted thither by desire
    To be Beauty's sacrifice.

But, Pity, on thy sable hearse
    Mine eyes the tears of sorrow shed ;
What though tears cannot fate reverse,
    Yet are they duties to the dead.
O, Mistress, in thy sanctuary
    Why wouldst thou suffer cold Disdain
To use his frozen cruelty,
    And gentle Pity to be slain ?

Pity that to thy Beauty fled,
    And with thy Beauty should have lived,
Ah, in thy heart lies buried,
    And nevermore may be revived :
Yet this last favour, dear, extend,
    To accept these vows, these tears I shed,
Duties which I thy pilgrim send,
    To Beauty living, Pity dead.

From ROBERT JONES' *Ultimum
Vale or Third Book of Airs*
(1608).

SHALL I look to ease my grief?
    No, my sight is lost with eying :
Shall I speak and beg relief?
    No, my voice is hoarse with crying :
    What remains but only dying?

Love and I of late did part,
    But the boy, my peace envỳing,
Like a Parthian threw his dart
    Backward, and did wound me flying :
    What remains but only dying ?

She whom then I looked on,
    My remembrance beautifying,
Stays with me though I am gone,
    Gone and at her mercy lying :
    What remains but only dying?

Shall I try her thoughts and write,
    No I have no means of trying :
If I should, yet at first sight
    She would answer with denying :
    What remains but only dying ?

Thus my vital breath doth waste,
    And, my blood with sorrow drying,
Sighs and tears make life to last
    For a while, their place supplying :
    What remains but only dying?

From WILLIAM BYRD'S *Songs of
Sundry Natures*, 1589.

1. WHO made thee, Hob, forsake the plough
       And fall in Love?
2. Sweet beauty, which hath power to bow
       The gods above.
1. What dost thou serve? 2. A shepherdess ;
       One such as hath no peer, I guess.
1. What is her name who bears thy heart
       Within her breast?
2. Silvana fair, of high desert,
       Whom I love best.
1. O, Hob, I fear she looks too high.
2. Yet love I must, or else I die.

From   RICHARD   CARLTON'S
Madrigals, 1601.

THE witless boy that blind is to behold,
   Yet blinded sees what in our fancy lies,
With smiling looks and hairs of curled gold
   Hath oft entrapped and oft deceived the wise :
No wit can serve his fancy to remove,
For finest wits are soonest thralled to Love.

From WILLIAM BYRD'S *Songs of Sundry Natures*, 1589.

WHILE that the sun with his beams hot
  Scorched the fruits in vale and mountain,
Philon, the shepherd, late forgot,
  Sitting beside a crystal fountain
    In shadow of a green oak-tree,
    Upon his pipe this song played he :
Adieu, Love ! adieu, Love ! untrue Love !
Untrue Love, untrue Love ! adieu, Love !
Your mind is light, soon lost for new love.

So long as I was in your sight,
  I was your heart, your soul, your treasure ;
And evermore you sobbed and sighed
  Burning in flames beyond all measure.
    Three days endured your love for me,
    And it was lost in other three.
Adieu, Love ! adieu, Love ! untrue Love !
Untrue Love, untrue Love ! adieu, Love !
Your mind is light, soon lost for new love.

Another shepherd you did see,
  To whom your heart was soon enchained ;
Full soon your love was leapt from me,
  Full soon my place he had obtained :
    Soon came a third your love to win ;
    And we were out, and he was in.
Adieu, Love ! adieu, Love ! untrue Love !
Untrue Love, untrue Love ! adieu, Love !
Your mind is light, soon lost for new love.

Sure, you have made me passing glad
   That you your mind so soon removed,
Before that I the leisure had
   To choose you for my best beloved :
      For all my love was passed and done
      Two days, before it was begun.
Adieu, Love ! adieu, Love ! untrue Love !
Untrue Love, untrue Love ! adieu, Love !
Your mind is light, soon lost for new love.

From JOHN WILBYE'S *First Set of
English Madrigals*, 1598.

A Y me, can every rumour
   Thus start my lady's humour ?
Name ye some galante to her,
Why straight forsooth I woo her.
Then burst[s] she forth in passion
" You men love but for fashion ; "
Yet sure I am that no man
Ever so loved woman.
Then alas, Love, be wary,
For women be contrary.

From CAMPION and ROSSETER'S
Book of Airs, 1601.

HARK, all you ladies that do sleep !
 The fairy-queen Proserpina
Bids you awake and pity them that weep :
 You may do in the dark
  What the day doth forbid ;
 Fear not the dogs that bark,
  Night will have all hid.

But if you let your lovers moan,
 The fairy-queen Proserpina
Will send abroad her fairies every one,
 That shall pinch black and blue
  Your white hands and fair arms
 That did not kindly rue
  Your paramours' [1] harms.

In myrtle arbours on the downs
 The fairy-queen Proserpina,
This night by moonshine leading merry rounds,
 Holds a watch with sweet love,
  Down the dale, up the hill ;
 No plaints or groans may move
  Their holy vigil.

1 " Paramour "=lover. (The word was frequently used in an
inoffensive sense.)

All you that will hold watch with love,
 The fairy-queen Proserpina
Will make you fairer than Dione's dove ;
 Roses red, lilies white,
  And the clear damask hue,
 Shall on your cheeks alight :
  Love will adorn you.

All you that love or loved before,
 The fairy-queen Proserpina
Bids you increase that loving humour more :
 They that yet have not fed
  On delight amorous,
 She vows that they shall lead
  Apes in Avernus.

From the Second Book of *Musica
Transalpina*, 1597.

BROWN is my Love, but graceful :
 And each renowned whiteness
Matched with thy lovely brown loseth its brightness.

 Fair is my Love, but scornful :
 Yet have I seen despised
Dainty white lilies, and sad flowers well prized.

From WILLIAM BYRD'S *Psalms,*
Sonnets, and Songs, 1588.

THE match that's made for just and true respects,
  With evenness both of years and parentage,
Of force must bring forth many good effects.
          Pari jugo dulcis tractus.

For where chaste love and liking sets the plant,
And concord waters with a firm good-will,
Of no good thing there can be any want.
          Pari jugo dulcis tractus.

Sound is the knot that Chastity hath tied,
Sweet is the music Unity doth make,
Sure is the store that Plenty doth provide.
          Pari jugo dulcis tractus.

Where Chasteness fails there Concord will decay,
Where Concord fleets there Plenty will decease,
Where Plenty wants there Love will wear away.
          Pari jugo dulcis tractus.

I, Chastity, restrain all strange desires ;
I, Concord, keep the course of sound consent ;
I, Plenty, spare and spend as cause requires.
          Pari jugo dulcis tractus.

Make much of us, all ye that married be ;
Speak well of us, all ye that mind to be ;
The time may come to want and wish all three.
                    Pari jugo dulcis tractus.

From WALTER PORTER's *Ma-
drigals and Airs,* 1632.

L OVE in thy youth, fair maid ; be wise,
    Old Time will make thee colder,
And though each morning new arise
    Yet we each day grow older.
Thou as heaven art fair and young,
    Thine eyes like twin stars shining :
But ere another day be sprung,
    All these will be declining.
Then winter comes with all his fears
    And all thy sweets shall borrow ;
Too late then wilt thou shower thy tears,
    And I too late shall sorrow.

From ROBERT JONES' *Musical
Dream,* 1609.

AND is it night? are they thine eyes that shine?
   Are we alone, and here? and here, alone?
May I come near, may I but touch thy shrine?
   Is jealousy asleep, and is he gone?
O Gods, no more! silence my lips with thine!
Lips, kisses, joys, hap, blessing most divine!

O come, my dear! our griefs are turned to night,
   And night to joys; night blinds pale envy's eyes;
Silence and sleep prepare us our delight;
   O cease we then our woes, our griefs, our cries:
O vanish words! words do but passions move;
O dearest life! joy's sweet! O sweetest love!

From FARMER'S *First Set of
English Madrigals,* 1599.

TAKE time while time doth last,
   Mark how fair[1] fadeth fast;
Beware if envy reign,
Take heed of proud disdain;
Hold fast now in thy youth,
Regard thy vowed truth,
Lest, when thou waxeth old,
Friends fail and love grow cold.

   [1] Fairness, beauty.

DIVINE AND MORAL POEMS.

From ROBERT JONES' *Musical
Dream*, 1609.

WHEN I sit reading all alone that secret book
　　Wherein I sigh to look,
How many spots there be
I wish I could not see,
Or from myself might flee !

Mine eyes for refuge then with zeal befix the skies,
My tears do cloud those eyes,
My sighs do blow them dry ;
And yet I live to die,
Myself I cannot fly.

Heavens, I implore, that knows my fault, what shall I
　　　do ?
To Hell I dare not go ;
The world first made me rue,
My self my griefs renew :
To whom then shall I sue ?

Alas, my soul doth faint to draw this doubtful breath .
Is there no hope in death ?
O yes, death ends my woes,
Death me from me will loose ,
My self am all my foes.

From THOMAS CAMPION'S *Two
Books of Airs* (circ. 1613).

VIEW me, Lord, a work of Thine !
   Shall I then lie drowned in night ?
Might Thy grace in me but shine,
   I should seem made all of light.

But my soul still surfeits so
   On the poisoned baits of sin
That I strange and ugly grow ;
   All is dark and foul within.

Cleanse me, Lord, that I may kneel
   At thine altar pure and white :
They that once Thy mercies feel,
   Gaze no more on earth's delight.

Worldly joys like shadows fade
   When the heavenly light appears :
But the covenants Thou hast made,
   Endless, know nor days nor years.

In Thy Word, Lord, is my trust,
   To Thy mercies fast I fly ;
Though I am but clay and dust,
   Yet Thy grace can lift me high.

From THOMAS CAMPION'S *Two
Books of Airs* (circ. 1613).

AWAKE, awake ! thou heavy sprite
    That sleep'st the deadly sleep of sin !
Rise now and walk the ways of light,
    'Tis not too late yet to begin.
Seek heaven early, seek it late ;
True Faith finds still an open gate.

Get up, get up, thou leaden man !
    Thy track, to endless joy or pain,
Yields but the model of a span :
    Yet burns out thy life's lamp in vain !
One minute bounds thy bane or bliss ;
Then watch and labour while time is.

From *Christ Church MS. I. 4. 78.*

TURN in, my Lord, turn into me,
    My heart's a homely place ;
But thou canst make corruption flee
And fill it with thy grace :
So furnished it will be brave,
And a rich dwelling thou shalt have.

From THOMAS CAMPION'S *Two
Books of Airs* (circ. 1613).

L O, when back mine eye,
  Pilgrim-like I cast,
What fearful ways I spy,
Which, blinded, I securely past !

But now heaven hath drawn
  From my brows that night ;
As when the day doth dawn,
So clears my long-imprisoned sight.

Straight the Caves of Hell
  Dressed with flowers I see,
Wherein False Pleasures dwell,
That, winning most, most deadly be.

Throngs of masked fiends
  Winged like angels, fly ;
Even in the gates of friends
In fair disguise black dangers lie.

Straight to heaven I raised
  My restored sight,
And with loud voice I praised
The Lord of ever-during light.

And since I had strayed
  From His ways so wide :
His grace I humbly prayed
Henceforth to be my guard and guide

N

From RICHARD CARLTON'S
Madrigals, 1601.

CONTENT thyself with thy estate,
    Seek not to climb above the skies,
For often love is mixed with hate
    And 'twixt the flowers the serpent lies :
Where fortune sends her greatest joys,
There once possest they are but toys.

What thing can earthly pleasure give
    That breeds delight when it is past ?
Or who so quietly doth live
    But storms of care do drown at last ?
This is the loan of worldly hire,
The more we have the more desire.

Wherefore I hold him best at ease
    That lives content with his estate,
And doth not sail in worldly seas
    Where Mine and Thine do breed debate :
This noble mind, even in a clown,
Is more than to possess a crown.

From JOHN DANYEL's *Songs for
the Lute, Viol, and Voice,*
1606.

IF I could shut the gate against my thoughts
 And keep out sorrow from this room within,
Or memory could cancel all the notes
 Of my misdeeds, and I unthink my sin :
How free, how clear, how clean my soul should lie,
Discharged of such a loathsome company !

Or were there other rooms without my heart
 That did not to my conscience join so near,
Where I might lodge the thoughts of sin apart
 That I might not their clam'rous crying hear ;
What peace, what joy, what ease should I possess,
Freed from their horrors that my soul oppress !

But, O my Saviour, who my refuge art,
 Let thy dear mercies stand 'twixt them and me,
And be the wall to separate my heart
 So that I may at length repose me free ;
That peace, and joy, and rest may be within,
And I remain divided from my sin.

From CAMPION and ROSSETER'S
Book of Airs, 1601.

THE man of life upright,
　Whose guiltless heart is free
From all dishonest deeds,
　Or thought of vanity ;

The man whose silent days
　In harmless joys are spent,
Whom hopes cannot delude
　Nor sorrow discontent :

That man needs neither towers
　Nor armour for defence,
Nor secret vaults to fly
　From thunder's violence :

He only can behold
　With unaffrighted eyes
The horrors of the deep
　And terrors of the skies.

Thus scorning all the cares
　That fate or fortune brings,
He makes the heaven his book,
　His wisdom heavenly things ;

Good thoughts his only friends,
　His wealth a well-spent age,
The earth his sober inn
　And quiet pilgrimage.

From THOMAS CAMPION'S *Two
Books of Airs* (circ. 1613).

TO music bent is my retired mind
 And fain would I some song of pleasure sing,
But in vain joys no comfort now I find ;
From heavenly thoughts all true delight doth spring :
Thy power, O God, Thy mercies to record,
Will sweeten every note and every word.

All earthly pomp or beauty to express
Is but to carve in snow, on waves to write ;
Celestial things, though men conceive them less,
Yet fullest are they in themselves of light :
Such beams they yield as know no means to die,
Such heat they cast as lifts the spirit high.

From WILLIAM BYRD'S *Psalms,
Songs, and Sonnets,* 1611.

LET not the sluggish sleep
 Close up thy waking eye,
Until with judgment deep
 Thy daily deeds thou try :
He that one sin in conscience keeps
 When he to quiet goes,
More vent'rous is than he that sleeps
 With twenty mortal foes.

From THOMAS GREAVES' *Songs
of Sundry Kinds,* 1604.

LET dread of pain for sin in after-time,
   Let shame to see thyself ensnared so,
Let grief conceived for foul accursed crime,
   Let hate of sin the worker of thy woe,
With dread, with shame, with grief, with hate enforce
To dew thy cheeks with tears of deep remorse.

So hate of sin shall cause God's love to grow,
   So grief shall harbour hope within thy heart,
So dread shall cause the flood of joy to flow,
   So shame shall send sweet solace to thy smart :
So love, so hope, so joy, so solace sweet
Shall make thy soul in heavenly bliss to fleet.[1]

Woe where such hate doth no such love allure !
   Woe where such grief doth make no hope proceed !
Woe where such dread doth no such joy procure !
   Woe where such shame doth no such solace breed !
Woe where no hate, no grief, no dread, no shame,
Doth neither love, hope, joy, or solace frame !

[1] Float.

From JOHN WILBYE'S *Second Set
of Madrigals,* 1609.

I LIVE, and yet methinks I do not breathe ;
  I thirst and drink, I drink and thirst again ;
I sleep and yet do dream I am awake ;
I hope for that I have ; I have and want :
I sing and sigh ; I love and hate at once.
  O, tell me restless soul, what uncouth jar
  Doth cause in store such want, in peace such war ?

Risposta.

There is a jewel which no Indian mines
Can buy, no chymic art can counterfeit ;
It makes men rich in greatest poverty ;
Makes water wine, turns wooden cups to gold,
The homely whistle to sweet music's strain :
  Seldom it comes, to few from heaven sent,
  That much in little, all in nought,—Content.

From WILLIAM BYRD'S *Songs of
Sundry Natures,* 1589.

IF in thine heart thou nourish ill,
  And give all to thy lust,
Then sorrows sharp and griefs at length
  Endure of force thou must :
But if that reason rule thy will,
  And govern all thy mind,
A blessed life then shalt thou lead
  And fewest dangers find.

From ROBERT JONES' *Ultimum
Vale, or Third Book of Airs,*
1608.

H APPY he
        Who, to sweet home retired,
    Shuns glory so admired,
        And to himself lives free,
Whilst he who strives with pride to climb the skies
Falls down with foul disgrace before he rise.

        Let who will
    The active life commend
    And all his travels bend
        Earth with his fame to fill :
Such fame, so forced, at last dies with his death,
Which life maintained by others' idle breath.

        My delights,
    To dearest home confined,
    Shall there make good my mind
        Not awed with fortune's spites :
High trees heaven blasts, winds shake and honors[1] fell,
When lowly plants long time in safety dwell.

        All I can,
    My worldly strife shall be
    They one day say of me
        ' He died a good old man ' :
On his sad soul a heavy burden lies
Who, known to all, unknown to himself dies.

[1] Qy. " hammers " ?

From THOMAS CAMPION'S *Two
Books of Airs* (circ. 1613).

C OME, cheerful day, part of my life to me ;
    For while thou view'st me with thy fading light,
Part of my life doth still depart with thee,
    And I still onward haste to my last night :
Time's fatal wings do ever forward fly,
So every day we live a day we die.

But, O ye nights, ordained for barren rest,
    How are my days deprived of life in you,
When heavy sleep my soul hath dispossest,
    By feigned death life sweetly to renew !
Part of my life in that, you life deny :
So every day we live a day we die.

From WILLIAM BYRD'S *Psalms,
Songs, and Sonnets,* 1611.

I N crystal towers and turrets richly set
    With glitt'ring gems that shine against the sun,
In regal rooms of jasper and of jet,
    Content of mind not always likes to won ; [1]
But oftentimes it pleaseth her to stay
In simple cotes enclosed with walls of clay.

1 Dwell.

From WILLIAM BYRD'S *Psalms*,
Sonnets, and Songs, 1588.

CARE for thy soul as thing of greatest price,
  Made to the end to taste of power divine,
Devoid of guilt, abhorring sin and vice,
  Apt by God's grace to virtue to incline :
Care for it so that by thy reckless train
It be not brought to taste eternal pain.

Care for thy corps, but chiefly for soul's sake ;
  Cut off excess, sustaining food is best ;
To vanquish pride, but comely clothing take ;
  Seek after skill, deep ignorance detest :
Care so (I say) the flesh to feed and clothe,
That thou harm not thy soul and body both.

Care for the world, to do thy body right ;
  Rack not thy wit to win by wicked ways ;
Seek not to oppress the weak by wrongful might ;
  To pay thy due do banish all delays :
Care to dispend according to thy store,
And in like sort be mindful of the poor.

Care for thy soul as for thy chiefest stay ;
  Care for thy body for the soul's avail ;
Care for the world for body's help alway ;
  Care yet but so as virtue may prevail :
Care in such sort as thou beware of this—
Care keep thee not from heaven and heavenly bliss !

From *Christ Church MS. K. 3.
43-5.* (Music by THOMAS
FORD.)

YET[1] if his majesty our sovereign lord
    Should of his own accord
Friendly himself invite,
And say " I'll be your guest to morrow night,"
How should we stir ourselves, call and command
All hands to work ! " Let no man idle stand.
Set me fine Spanish tables in the hall,
    See they be fitted all ;
    Let there be room to eat,
And order taken that there want no meat.
See every sconce and candlestick made bright,
That without tapers they may give a light.
Look to the presence : are the carpets spread,
    The dais [2] o'er the head,
    The cushions in the chairs,
And all the candles lighted on the stairs ?
Perfume the chambers, and in any case
Let each man give attendance in his place."
Thus if the king were coming would we do,
    And 'twere good reason too ;
    For 'tis a duteous thing
To show all honour to an earthly king,
And after all our travail and our cost,
So he be pleased, to think no labour lost.

1 These verses seem to have been taken from some longer
poem.
2 MS. "dazie.

But at the coming of the King of Heaven
All's set at six and seven :
We wallow in our sin,
Christ cannot find a chamber in the inn.
We entertain him always like a stranger,
And as at first still lodge him in the manger.

TRISTIA.

From WILLIAM CORKINE'S
Second Book of Airs, 1612.

WHEN I was born Lucina cross-legged sate,
    The angry stars with ominous aspects
Frowned on my birth, and the foredooming Fate
    Ordained to brand me with their dire effects :
The sun did hide his face and left the night
To bring me to this world's accursed light.

From ROBERT JONES' *First Book
of Songs and Airs*, 1601.

LIE down, poor heart, and die awhile for grief,
    Think not this world will ever do thee good ;
Fortune forewarns thou look to thy relief,
    And sorrow sucks upon thy living blood :
Then this is all can help thee of this hell,
Lie down and die, and then thou shalt do well.

Day gives his light but to thy labours' toil,
    And night her rest but to thy weary bones ;
Thy fairest fortune's[1] followed with a foil,
    And laughing ends but with thine[2] after-groans :
And this is all can help thee of thy hell,
Lie down and die, and then thou shalt do well.

From JOHN DOWLAND'S *A Pilgrim's Solace,* 1612.

GO, nightly cares, the enemy to rest,
    Forbear a while to vex my wearied sprite ;
So long your weight hath lain upon my breast
That, lo ! I live of life bereaved quite :
O give me time to draw my wearied breath,
Or let me die as I desire the death.
Welcome, sweet Death ! O life, no life, a hell !
Then thus and thus I bid the world farewell.

False world, farewell, the enemy to rest,
Now do thy worst, I do not weigh thy spite ;
Free from thy cares I live for ever blest,
Enjoying peace and heavenly true delight :
Delight, whom woes nor sorrows shall amate,[3]
Nor fears or tears disturb her happy state :
And thus I leave thy hopes, thy joys untrue,
And thus, and thus, vain world, again adieu !

---

[1] Old ed. "fortune followes."   [2] Old ed. "their."
[3] Confound.

From THOMAS MORLEY'S *The First Book of Airs*, 1600.

COME, Sorrow, come, sit down and mourn with me ;
  Hang down thy head upon thy baleful breast,
That God and man and all the world may see
Our heavy hearts do live in quiet rest :
Enfold thine arms and wring thy wretched hands
To shew the state wherein poor Sorrow stands.

Cry not outright, for that were children's guise,
But let thy tears fall trickling down thy face,
And weep so long until thy blubbered eyes
May see in sum [1] the depth of thy disgrace.
Oh shake thy head, but not a word but mum ;
The heart once dead, the tongue is stroken dumb.

And let our fare be dishes of despite
To break our hearts and not our fasts withal ;
Then let us sup with sorrow-sops at night,
And bitter sauce all of a broken gall :
Thus let us live till heavens may rue to see
The doleful doom ordained for thee and me.

[1] Old ed. "May see (in Sunne)."

From JOHN DOWLAND'S *Second*
Book of Songs or Airs, 1600.

COME, ye heavy states of night,
　Do my father's spirit right ;
Soundings baleful let me borrow,
Burthening my song with sorrow.
　　Come, Sorrow, come ! her eyes that sings
　　By thee are turned into springs.

Come, you virgins of the night,
That in dirges sad delight,
Quire my anthems : I do borrow
Gold nor pearl, but sounds of sorrow.
　　Come, Sorrow, come ! her eyes that sings
　　By thee are turned into springs.

From JOHN WILBYE'S *Second Set*
of Madrigals, 1609.

DRAW on, sweet Night, best friend unto those
　　cares
　That do arise from painful melancholy ;
My life so ill through want of comfort fares,
　That unto thee I consecrate it wholly.

Sweet Night, draw on ; my griefs, when they be told
　To shades and darkness, find some ease from paining ;
And while thou all in silence dost enfold,
　I then shall have best time for my complaining.

From CAMPION and ROSSETER'S
Book of Airs, 1601.

THE cypress curtain of the night is spread,
    And over all a silent dew is cast ;
The weaker cares by sleep are conquered,
    But I alone, with hideous grief aghast,
In spite of Morpheus' charms a watch do keep
Over mine eyes, to banish careless sleep.

Yet oft my trembling eyes through faintness close,
    And then the Map of Hell before me stands,
Which ghosts do see, and I am one of those
    Ordained to pine in sorrow's endless bands ;
Since from my wretched soul all hopes are reft,
And now no cause of life to me is left.

Grief, seize my soul ! for that will still endure
    When my crazed body is consumed and gone :
Bear it to thy black den, there keep it sure,
    Where thou ten thousand souls dost tire upon :
Yet all do not afford such food to thee
As this poor one, the worser part of me.

From JOHN MUNDY'S *Songs and Psalms*, 1594. (Words ascribed to CHYDIOCK TYCHBOURNE.)

M Y prime of youth is but a frost of cares ;
    My feast of joy is but a dish of pain ;
My crop of corn is but a field of tares ;
    And all my good is but vain hope of gain ;
My life is fled, and yet I saw no sun ;
And now I live, and now my life is done.

The spring is past, and yet it hath not sprung ;
    The fruit is dead, and yet the leaves be green ;
My youth is gone, and yet I am but young ;
    I saw the world and yet I was not seen ;
My thread is cut, and yet it is not spun ;
And now I live, and now my life is done.

VARIA.

From *Christ Church MS. I.* 5. 49.

H EH nonny no !
   Men are fools that wish to die !
Is't not fine to dance and sing
When the bells of death do ring?
Is't not fine to swim in wine,
And turn upon the toe
And sing hey nonny no,
When the winds blow and the seas flow?
Hey nonny no !

From THOMAS VAUTOR'S *Songs
of divers Airs and Natures,*
1619.

S WEET Suffolk owl, so trimly dight
   With feathers like a lady bright,
Thou sing'st alone, sitting by night,
    Te whit, te whoo !
Thy note, that forth so freely rolls,
With shrill command the mouse controls,
And sings a dirge for dying souls,
    Te whit, te whoo !

From THOMAS CAMPION'S *The Description of a Masque presented before the King's Majesty at Whitehall,* 1607.

NEITHER buskin now, nor bays,
   Challenge I ; a lady's praise
Shall content my proudest hope :
Their applause was all my scope,
And to their shrines properly
Revels dedicated be :
Whose soft ears none ought to pierce
But with smooth and gentle verse.
Let the tragic poem swell,
Raising raging fiends from hell;
And let epic dactyls range
Swelling seas and countries strange :
Little room small things contains,
Easy praise quits easy pains.
Suffer them whose brows do sweat
To gain honour by the great ; [1]
It's enough if men me name
A retailer of such fame.

   1 " By the great,"—wholesale.

From THOMAS CAMPION'S *Two
Books of Airs* (circ. 1613).

JACK and Joan, they think no ill,
    But loving live, and merry still;
Do their week-days' work, and pray
Devoutly on the holy day:
Skip and trip it on the green,
And help to choose the Summer Queen;
Lash out at a country feast
 Their silver penny with the best.

Well can they judge of nappy ale,
And tell at large a winter tale;
Climb up to the apple loft,
And turn the crabs till they be soft.
Tib is all the father's joy,
And little Tom the mother's boy.
All their pleasure is Content;
And care, to pay their yearly rent.

Joan can call by name her cows
And deck her windows with green boughs;
She can wreaths and tutties [1] make,
And trim with plums a bridal cake.
Jack knows what brings gain or loss;
And his long flail can stoutly toss:
Makes the hedge which others break,
And ever thinks what he doth speak.

       1 Nosegays.

Now, you courtly dames and knights,
That study only strange delights ;
Though you scorn the homespun gray
And revel in your rich array ;
Though your tongues dissemble deep,
And can your heads from danger keep ;
Yet, for all your pomp and train,
Securer lives the silly swain.

From THOMAS BATESON'S *First
Set of English Madrigals*
1604.

SISTER, awake ! close not your eyes !
     The day her light discloses,
And the bright morning doth arise
     Out of her bed of roses.

See, the clear sun, the world's bright eye,
     In at our window peeping :
Lo ! how he blusheth to espy
     Us idle wenches sleeping.

Therefore, awake ! make haste, I say,
     And let us, without staying,
All in our gowns of green so gay
     Into the park a-maying.

From THOMAS CAMPION'S *Fourth Book of Airs* (circ. 1617).

TO his sweet lute Apollo sang the motions of the
    spheres,
The wondrous orders of the stars whose course divides
    the years,
      And all the mysteries above ;
      But none of this could Midas move :
Which purchased him his ass's ears.

Then Pan with his rude pipe began the country wealth
    t' advance,
To boast of cattle, flocks of sheep, and goats on hills
    that dance,
      With much more of this churlish kind,
      That quite transported Midas' mind,
And held him rapt as in a trance.

This wrong the God of Music scorned from such a
    sottish judge,
And bent his angry bow at Pan, which made the
    piper trudge :
      Then Midas' head he did so trim
      That every age yet talks of him
And Phœbus' right revenged grudge.

From Thomas Campion's *Third
Book of Airs* (circ. 1617).

NOW winter nights enlarge
   The number of their hours,
And clouds their storms discharge
Upon the airy towers.
Let now the chimneys blaze,
And cups o'erflow with wine ;
Let well-tuned words amaze
With harmony divine.
Now yellow waxen lights
Shall wait on honey love,
While youthful revels, masques, and courtly sights
Sleep's leaden spells remove.

This time doth well dispense
With lovers' long discourse ;
Much speech hath some defence,
Though beauty no remorse.
All do not all things well ;
Some measures comely tread,
Some knotted riddles tell,
Some poems smoothly read.
The summer hath his joys
And winter his delights ;
Though love and all his pleasures are but toys,
They shorten tedious nights.

From *Gesta Graiorum: Gray's
Inn Masque,* 1594. (By
THOMAS CAMPION.)

A HYMN IN PRAISE OF NEPTUNE.

OF Neptune's empire let us sing,
  At whose command the waves obey ;
To whom the rivers tribute pay,
Down the high mountains sliding :
To whom the scaly nation yields
Homage for the crystal fields
    Wherein they dwell :
And every sea-god pays a gem
Yearly out of his wat'ry cell
To deck great Neptune's diadem.

The Tritons dancing in a ring,
Before his palace-gates do make
The water with their echoes quake,
Like the great thunder sounding :
The sea-nymphs chant their accents shrill,
And the sirens, taught to kill
    With their sweet voice,
Make ev'ry echoing rock reply,
Unto their gentle murmuring noise,
The praise of Neptune's empery.

From THOMAS RAVENSCROFT'S
Melismata, 1611.

THE MARRIAGE OF THE FROG AND THE MOUSE.

IT was the frog in the well,
    Humbledum, humbledum,
And the merry mouse in the mill,
        Tweedle, tweedle, twino.

The frog would a-wooing ride
Sword and buckler by his side.

When he upon his high horse set,
His boots they shone as black as jet.

When he came to the merry mill-pin,—
"Lady Mouse, been you within?"

Then came out the dusty mouse:
"I am Lady of this house:

Hast thou any mind of me?"
"I have e'en great mind of thee?"

"Who shall this marriage make?"
"Our Lord which is the rat."

"What shall we have to our supper?"
"Three beans in a pound of butter?"

When supper they were at,
The frog, the mouse, and e'en the rat ;

Then came in Gib our cat,
And catched the mouse e'en by the back.

Then did they separate,
And the frog leaped on the floor so flat.

Then came in Dick our drake,
And drew the frog e'en to the lake.

The rat run up the wall,
    Humbledum, humbledum ;
A goodly company, the Devil go with all !
    Tweedle tweedle twino.

From Melismata, 1611.

THE BELLMAN'S SONG.

MAIDS to bed and cover coal ;
    Let the mouse out of her hole ;
Crickets in the chimney sing
Whilst the little bell doth ring :
If fast asleep, who can tell
When the clapper hits the bell?

From *Christ Church MS. I.* 5.
49. (Music by ALFONSO
FERRABOSCO.)

THERE was a frog swum in the lake,
  The crab came crawling by :
"Wilt thou," coth the frog, "be my make [1] ?"
Coth the crab "No, not I."
"My skin is sooth [2] and dappled fine,
I can leap far and nigh.
Thy shell is hard : so is not mine."
Coth the crab "No, not I."
"Tell me," then spake the crab, "therefore,
Or else I thee defy :
Give me thy claw, I ask no more."
Coth the frog, "That will I."
The crab bit off the frog's fore-feet ;
The frog then he must die.
To woo a crab it is not meet :
If any do, it is not I.

[1] The MS. gives "mate"; but I read "make" (an old form
of "mate") for the sake of the rhyme.
[2] S ft, sleek.

From THOMAS RAVENSCROFT'S
Brief Discourse, &c., 1614.

THE URCHINS' DANCE.

BY the moon we sport and play,
  With the night begins our day :
As we frisk the dew doth fall ;
Trip it, little urchins all !
Lightly as the little bee,
Two by two, and three by three ;
And about, about go we.

THE ELVES' DANCE.

Round about in a fair ring-a,
Thus we dance and thus we sing-a ;
Trip and go, to and fro,
Over this green-a ;
All about, in and out,
Over this green-a.

THE FAIRIES' DANCE.

DARE you haunt our hallow'd green ?
  None but fairies here are seen.
Down and sleep,
Wake and weep,
Pinch him black, and pinch him blue,
That seeks to steal a lover true !
When you come to hear us sing,
Or to tread our fairy ring,
Pinch him black, and pinch him blue !
O thus our nails shall handle you !

The Satyrs' Dance.

ROUND-A, round-a, keep your ring :
To the glorious sun we sing,—
Ho, ho !
He that wears the flaming rays,
And th' imperial crown of bays,
Him with shouts and songs we praise—
Ho, ho !
That in his bounty he'd vouchsafe to grace
The humble sylvans and their shaggy race.

From GEORGE MASON's and JOHN
EARSDEN's *Airs that were
sung and played at Brougham
Castle in Westmoreland in the
King's Entertainment given
by the Earl of Cumberland,*
1618.

LET us in a lover's round
Circle all this hallowed ground ;
Softly, softly trip and go,
The light-foot Fairies jet it so.
Forward then, and back again,
Here and there and everywhere,
Winding to and fro,
Skipping high and louting low ;
And, like lovers, hand in hand,
March around and make a stand.

From MARTIN PEERSON'S *Private Music*, 1620. (Words by ROBERT VERSTEGAN.)

UPON my lap my sovereign sits
   And sucks upon my breast ;
Meantime his love maintains my life
And gives my sense her rest.
   Sing lullaby, my little boy,
   Sing lullaby, mine only joy !

When thou hast taken thy repast,
Repose, my babe, on me ;
So may thy mother and thy nurse
Thy cradle also be.
   Sing lullaby, my little boy,
   Sing lullaby, mine only joy !

I grieve that duty doth not work
All that my wishing would,
Because I would not be to thee
But in the best I should.
   Sing lullaby, my little boy,
   Sing lullaby, mine only joy !

Yet as I am, and as I may,
I must and will be thine,
Though all too little for thy self
Vouchsafing to be mine.
   Sing lullaby, my little boy,
   Sing lullaby, mine only joy !

WHAT pleasure have great princes
   More dainty to their choice
Than herdsmen wild, who careless
In quiet life rejoice,
And fortune's fate not fearing
Sing sweet in summer morning?

Their dealings plain and rightful,
Are void of all deceit ;
They never know how spiteful,
It is to kneel and wait
On favourite presumptuous
Whose pride is vain and sumptuous.

All day their flocks each tendeth ;
At night, they take their rest ;
More quiet than who sendeth
His ship into the East,
Where gold and pearl are plenty ;
But getting, very dainty.

For lawyers and their pleading,
They 'steem it not a straw ;
They think that honest meaning
Is of itself a law :
Whence conscience judgeth plainly,
They spend no money vainly.

O happy who thus liveth !
Not caring much for gold ;
With clothing which sufficeth
To keep him from the cold.
Though poor and plain his diet
Yet merry it is, and quiet.

From THOMAS WEELKES' *Airs or Fantastic Spirits*, 1608.

HA ha ! ha ha ! this world doth pass
    Most merrily, I'll be sworn ;
For many an honest Indian ass
    Goes for an Unicorn.
             Farra diddle dino ;
             This is idle fino.

Ty hye ! ty hye ! O sweet delight !
    He tickles this age that can
Call Tullia's ape a marmosyte
    And Leda's goose a swan.
             Farra diddle dino ;
             This is idle fino.

So so ! so so ! fine English days !
    When false play's no reproach :
For he that doth the coachman praise,
    May safely use the coach.
             Farra diddle dino ;
             This is idle fino.

P

From Thomas Weelkes' *Madrigals of Six Parts*, 1600.

A SPARROW-HAWK proud did hold in wicked
  jail
Music's sweet chorister, the nightingale,
To whom with sighs she said : " O set me free !
And in my song I'll praise no bird but thee."
The hawk replied, " I will not lose my diet
To let a thousand such enjoy their quiet."

From Thomas Morley's *First
Book of Ballets*, 1595.

NOW is the month of maying,
  When merry lads are playing
Each with his bonny lass
Upon the greeny grass.
                Fa la la !

The spring clad all in gladness
Doth laugh at winter's sadness,
And to the bagpipe's sound
The nymphs tread out their ground.
                Fa la la !

Fie then, why sit we musing,
Youth's sweet delight refusing?
Say, dainty nymphs, and speak,
Shall we play barley-break.
                Fa la la !

From Thomas Morley's *First
Book of Ballets,* 1595.

SING we and chant it
While love doth grant it,
Fa la la !

Not long youth lasteth
And old age hasteth.
Fa la la !

Now is best leisure
To take our pleasure.
Fa la la !

All things invite us
Now to delight us.
Fa la la !

Hence care be packing,
No mirth be lacking.
Fa la la !

Let spare no treasure
To live in pleasure.
Fa la la !

From THOMAS CAMPION'S *Fourth Book of Airs* (circ. 1617).

EVERY dame affects good fame, whate'er her doings be,
But true praise is Virtue's bays, which none may wear but she.
Borrowed guise fits not the wise, a simple look is best;
Native grace becomes a face though ne'er so rudely drest.
Now such new-found toys are sold these women to disguise,
That before the year grows old the newest fashion dies.

Dames of yore contended more in goodness to exceed,
Than in pride to be envied for that which least they need.
Little lawn then serve[d] the Pawn, if Pawn at all there were;
Homespun thread and household bread then held out all the year.
But th' attires of women now wear out both house and land;
That the wives in silk may flow, at ebb the good men stand.

Once again, Astræa! then from heaven to earth descend,
And vouchsafe in their behalf these errors to amend.

Aid from heaven must make all even, things are so out
  of frame ;
For let man strive all he can, he needs must please his
  dame.
Happy man, content that gives and what he gives
  enjoys !
Happy dame, content that lives and breaks no sleep
  for toys !

From CAMPION and ROSSETER'S
Book of Airs, 1601.

WHETHER men do laugh or weep,
  Whether they do wake or sleep,
Whether they die young or old,
Whether they feel heat or cold ;
There is underneath the sun
Nothing in true earnest done.

All our pride is but a jest,
None are worst and none are best ;
Grief and joy and hope and fear
Play their pageants everywhere :
Vain Opinion all doth sway,
And the world is but a play.

Powers above in clouds do sit,
Mocking our poor apish wit,
That so lamely with such state
Their high glory imitate.
No ill can be felt but pain,
And that happy men disdain.

NOTES.

NOTES.

Page 2. "At her fair hands."—This poem had appeared in Francis Davison's *Poetical Rhapsody*. It belongs to Walter Davison, younger brother of Francis.

Page 4. "Come, you pretty false-eyed wanton."— Occasionally Campion does not know where to stop. I have ventured to suppress the third stanza, but restore it in the notes :—

> "Would it were dumb midnight now,
>   When all the world lies sleeping !
> Would this place some desert were,
>   Which no man hath in keeping !
> My desires should then be safe,
>   And when you cried, then would I laugh :
> But if ought might breed offence,
>   Love only should be blamed :
> I would live your servant still,
>   And you my saint unnamed."

The poem reads better without it.

Page 10. "My Thoughts are winged with Hopes."— In *England's Helicon*. A MS. copy in a commonplace book found at Hamburg is signed "W.S." There is not the slightest ground for identifying "W. S." with Shakespeare.

Page 11. " It was the purest light of heaven for whose fair love they fell."—I am reminded of a fine passage in Drayton's *Barons' Wars*, canto vi. :—

> " Looking upon proud Phaeton wrapped in fire,
> The gentle queen did much bewail his fall ;
> But Mortimer commended his desire
> To lose one poor life or to govern all.
> ' What though,' quoth he, ' he madly did aspire
> And his great mind made him proud Fortune's thrall ?
> Yet, in despight when she her worst had done,
> *He perished in the chariot of the sun.*' "

Page 14. " The sun still *proved*" (last line).—Here, as frequently, *proved = approved.* (A correspondent suggests that *proved* may be a misprint for *proud*).

Page 17. " From Citheron the warlike boy is fled." —Elizabethan poets were fond of putting *Citheron* for *Cythera.*

Page 18. " That kisses were the *seals of love.*"— Every reader will recall Shakespeare's

> " But my kisses bring again, bring again,
> *Seals of love* but sealed in vain, sealed in vain."

(The first stansa is found among the poems "of sundrie other Noblemen and Gentlemen" appended to the surreptitious edition of Sir Philip Sidney's *Astrophel and Stella*, 1591).

Page 31. " There is a lady sweet and kind."— Printed in *The Golden Garland of Princely Delights*, 1620, and other collections.

Page 32. This song is found with considerable variations in William Corkine's *Airs*, 1610, where only three stanzas are given :—

" Think you to seduce me so with words that have no meaning?
Parrots can learn so to speak, our voice by pieces gleaning :
Nurses teach their children so about the time of weaning.

" Learn to speak first, then to woo, to wooing much pertaineth :
He that hath not heart to hide, soon falters when he feigneth,
And, as one that wants his wits, he smiles when he complaineth.

" If with wit we be deceived our faults may be excused,
Seeming good with flattery graced is but of few refused,
But of all accursed are they that are by fools abused."

Page 33. " Thou art not fair for all thy red and white."
—There are two other versions of this poem (which
has been erroneously attributed to Dr. Donne and to
Joshua Sylvester) in Harl. MS. 6910, fol. 150 (written
circ. 1596).

" Thou shalt not love me, neither shall these eyes
Shine on my soul shrouded in deadly night ;
Thou shalt not breathe on me thy spiceries,
Nor rock me in thy quavers of delight.
Hold off thy hands ; for I had rather die
Than have my life by thy coy touch reprieved.
Smile not on me, but frown thou bitterly :
Slay me outright, no lovers are long lived.
As for those lips reserved so much in store,
Their rosy verdure shall not meet with mine.
Withhold thy proud embracements evermore :
I'll not be swaddled in those arms of thine.
    Now show it if thou be a woman right,—
    Embrace and kiss and love me in despight."
                    Finis. Tho: Camp :

" BEAUTY WITHOUT LOVE DEFORMITY.

" Thou art not fair for all thy red and white,
For all those rosy temperatures in thee ;
Thou art not sweet, though made of mere delight,
Nor fair nor sweet unless thou pity me.
Thine eyes are black, and yet their glittering brightness
Can night enlumine in her darkest den ;

> Thy hands are bloody, though ¹ contrived of whiteness,
> Both black and bloody, if they murder men ;
> Thy brows whereon my good hap doth depend,
> Fairer than snow or lily in the spring ;
> Thy tongue which saves (?) at every sweet word's end,
> That hard as marble, this a mortal sting :
> I will not soothe thy follies, thou shalt prove
> That Beauty is no Beauty without Love."
>
> *Finis. Idem.*

Page 34. "Though Amaryllis dance in green."—
These lines are also in *England's Helicon,* 1600.

Page 36. " What poor astronomers are they."—This
poem has been ascribed, without evidence, to Nicholas
Breton.

Page 39. "Silly boy,'tis full moon yet," &c.—Horace's
ode to Pyrrha must have been in Campion's mind when
he wrote this delightful lyric.

Page 40. " Since first I saw your face I resolved,"
&c.—Found in the *Golden Garland of Princely
Delights,* and other collections.

Page 45. " Thrice toss these oaken ashes in the air."
—This poem was included in the 1633 edition of Joshua
Sylvester's works, among the " Remains never till now
imprinted." Sylvester has not a shadow of claim to it.
There is a MS. copy of it in Harleian MS. 6910, fol.
150, where it is correctly assigned to Campion. The
MS. gives it in the form of a sonnet :—

> " Thrice toss those oaken ashes in the air,
> And thrice three times tie up this true love's knot ;
> Thrice sit you down in this enchanted chair,
> And murmur soft " She will or she will not."
> Go, burn those poisoned weeds in that blue fire,
> This cypress gathered out a dead man's grave,

¹ MS. " thoughts."

These screech-owl's feathers and the prickling briar,
That all thy thorny cares an end may have.
Then come, you fairies, dance with me a round !
Dance in a circle, let my love be centre !
Melodiously breathe an enchanted sound :
Melt her hard heart that some remorse may enter !
In vain are all the charms I can devise ;
She hath an art to break them with her eyes."

Page 52. " Disdain me still."—Ascribed to Lord
Pembroke in the *Poems* of Pembroke and Ruddier
(1660) ; but the authorship is doubtful.

Page 64. " Lady, when I behold the roses sprouting."
—Gracefully paraphrased from an Italian madrigal
of Celiano :—

" Quand' io miro le rose,
Ch' in voi natura pose ;
E quelle che v' ha l'arte
Nel vago seno sparte ;
Non so conoscer poi
Se vol le rose, o sian le rose in voi."

There is another version of this madrigal (Mr. J. M.
Thomson reminds me) in Lodge's *William Longbeard*,
1593.

Page 68. " Those eyes that set my fancy," &c.—
A free rendering of Desportes' sonnet :—

" Du bel œil de Diane est my flamme empruntée,
En ses nœuds blon-dorez mon cœur est arresté," &c.

Page 71. " So saith my fair and beautiful Lycoris."—
This little poem and the next are renderings of an
Italian madrigal of Guarini.

Page 80. " There is a garden in her face."—This
poem is set to music in Alison's *Hour's Recreation*,
1606, and Robert Jones' *Ultimum Vale* (1608). Her-
rick's dainty verses, " Cherry ripe, ripe, ripe ! I cry,"
are too well known to bear repetition.

Page 87. " What needeth all this travail and turmoiling."—Compare Spenser's fifteenth sonnet :—

" Ye tradefull Merchants that with weary toyle
Do seeke most pretious things to make your gain
And both the Indias of their treasure spoile,
What needeth you to seeke so farre in vaine?
For loe ! my Love doth in her selfe containe
All this worlds riches that may farre be found.
If Saphyres, loe ! her eics be Saphyres plaine ;
If Rubies, loe ! hir lips be Rubies sound ;
If Pearles, hir teeth be pearles, both pure and round ;
If Yvorie her forehead yvory weene ;
If Gold, her locks be fairest gold on ground ;
If Silver, her faire hands are silver sheene :
　　But that which fairest is but few behold,
　　Her mind, adorned with vertues manifold."

Spenser here paraphrases a sonnet of Philippe Desportes beginning :—

" Marchans, qui traversez tout le rivage More,
Du froid Septentrion, et qui sans reposer
A cent mille dangers vous allez exposer," &c.

A certain " E. C.," in a dull volume of sonnets entitled
Emaricdulfe, 1595, has also imitated Desportes :—

" What meane our Merchants so with eger minds
To plough the seas to find rich iuels forth,
Sith in Emaricduffe a thousand kinds
Are heap'd, exceeding wealthie Indias worth ? " &c.

A unique copy of " E. C.'s " sonnets is preserved at
Lamport Hall, Northamptonshire, the seat of Sir
Charles Isham, Bart.

Page 91. " Whoever thinks or hopes of love for
love."—This poem is printed, with many alterations of
text, among the *Works*, 1633, of Fulke Greville, Lord
Brooke.

Page 94. " When thou must home to shades of

underground."—The mention of white Iope must have
been suggested by a passage of Propertius (ii. 28) :—

> "Sunt apud infernos tot millia formosarum ;
> Pulchra sit in superis, si licet, una locis.
> Vobiscum est Iope, vobiscum candida Tyro,
> Vobiscum Europe, nec proba Pasiphae."

Page 101. "If women could be fair and never
fond."—In Rawlinson MS. Poet. 85, fol. 16, this poem
is ascribed to Edward, Earl of Oxford.

Page 102. "My sweetest Lesbia, let us live and
love."—Suggested by, and partly translated from, Catullus'

> "Vivamus, mea Lesbia, atque amemus."

Page 104. "Now let her change."—This song is
also set to music in Robert Jones's *Ultimum Vale*
(1608).

Page 105. "Sweet Love, my only treasure."—This
is one of "A. W.'s" poems in Davison's *Poetical
Rhapsody*. It has yet to be discovered who "A. W."
was.

Page 120. "The lowest trees have tops, the ant her
gall."—This poem was printed in Davison's *Poetical
Rhapsody*, 1602, where it is subscribed "Incerto." In
Rawlinson MS. Poet. 148, fol. 50, it is attributed to
Sir Edward Dyer.

Page 121. "In the merry month of May."—First
printed, under the title of "The Ploughman's Song,"
in *The Honourable Entertainment given to the Queen's
Majesty in Progress at Elvetham in Hampshire, by
the Right Honorable the Earl of Hertford*, 1591.

Page 130. "Greedy lover, pause awhile."—In
Huth's *Inedited Poetical Miscellanies* this poem is

attributed on early MS. authority to Sir Albertus Morton, nephew of Sir Henry Wotton (who wrote a touching elegy on him). Morton died in 1625.

Page 133. "Cupid in a bed of roses."—Translated from Anacreon's ode "Ἔρως ποτ' ἐν ῥόδοισι."

Page 136. "*Women,* what are they?—*We men,* what are we?"—For the play on the words *women* and *we men,* cf. Peele's *Edward I.* :—

"*Lancaster.* Believe him not, sweet niece: *we men* can speak smooth for advantage.

Joan. Women, do you mean, my good uncle? Well, be the accent where it will, women are women."

Page 144. "Farewell, false Love, the oracle of lies." —"J. C." in *Alcilia,* 1595, writes :—

" Love is honey mixed with gall,
A thraldom free, a freedom thrall ;
A bitter sweet, a pleasant sour,
Got in a year, lost in an hour ;
A peaceful war, a warlike peace,
Whose wealth brings want, whose want increase ;
Full long pursuit and little gain,
Uncertain pleasure, certain pain ;
Regard of neither right nor wrong,
For short delights repentance long.

Love is the sickness of the thought,
Conceit of pleasure dearly bought ;
A restless passion of the mind,
A labyrinth of errors blind ;
A sugared poison, fair deceit,
A bait for fools, a furious heat ;
A chilling cold, a wondrous passion,
Exceeding man's imagination ;
Which none can tell in whole or part,
But only he that feels the smart."

Robert Greene has a somewhat similar description of Love ("What thing is Love? it is a power divine," &c.) in *Menaphon*, 1589.

Page 153. "Farewell, dear love! since thou wilt needs be gone."—It is to this song that allusion is made in *Twelfth Night*, ii. 3.

Page 156. "You say you love me."—By Robert Heath, the cavalier poet. See *Clarastella*, 1650, p. 23, "Clarastella distrusting."

Page 161. "On a time the amorous Silvy."—Gracefully rendered from the French of Pierre Guedron :—

> "Un jour l'amoureuse Silvie
> Disoit, baise moy, je te prie,
> Au berger qui seul est sa vie
> Et son amour :
> Baise moy, Pasteur, je te prie,
> Et te leve, car il est jour," &c.

Page 162. "Lais, now old," &c.—Imitated from Plato's epigram (*Anthol. Graec.* vi. 1) "Ἡ σοβαρὸν γελάσασα καθ' Ἑλλάδος," &c., or from Ausonius' translation "De Laide dicante Veneri speculum suum."

Page 167. "While that the sun with his beams hot." —Also printed in *England's Helicon*, 1600, 1614.

Page 172. "Love in thy youth, fair maid ; be wise." —I give this song from Beloe's *Anecdotes*, where it is said to be taken from Walter Porter's *Madrigals and Airs*, 1632. I have searched far and wide for the song-book, but have not yet been able to discover a copy. There is an early MS. copy of the present song in Ashmole MS. 38, No. 188.

Page 180. "The man of life upright."—This poem was reprinted, with some slight changes, in Campion's *Two Books of Airs,* circ. 1613. It has been erroneously attributed to Bacon.

Page 181. "Let not the sluggish sleep."—These verses form part of a longer poem appended to the *Interlude of Wit and Science* (Shakespeare Society, 1848, pp. 76-77).

Page 184. "Who, known to all, unknown to himself dies."—From Seneca's *Thyestes* :—

> " qui, notus nimis omnibus,
> Ignotus moritur sibi."

Page 189. "When I was born Lucina *cross-legged* sat," *i.e.* to prolong the pangs of child-birth and hinder the child's entrance to the world. Witches were often accused of sitting cross-legged at the door of travailing women.

Page 191. "Oh shake thy head, but *not a word but mum.*"—The expression *not a word but mum* (= silence) was proverbial. Cf. Peele's *Old Wives' Tale :*—

> " What? *not a word but mum?* then, Sacrapant,
> We are betrayed."

Page 194. "My prime of youth is but a frost of cares."—In *Reliquiæ Wottonianæ* this poem is said to have been written by "Chidick Tychborn, being young and then in the Tower, the night before his execution." Chidiock Tychbourne of Southampton was executed in 1586 with Ballard and Babington. The verses first appeared in a poetical tract printed at the time of Tychbourne's execution (*Huth's Fugitive Poetical Tracts,* first series, No. 26) ; they were set to music in Richard Alison's *Hour's Recreation,* 1606, and Michael Este's *Madrigals of three, four, and five Parts,* 1604.

Page 195. "Hey nonny no!"—In the MS. these sprightly verses are subscribed "Mr. Gyles." Nathaniel Giles was successively chorister at Magdalen, organist and master of the choristers at St. George's, Windsor, and master of the children of the Chapel Royal. He died 24 January, 1633, and was buried at Windsor.

Page 201. "Of Neptune's empire let us ˌsing."— These verses are printed in Davison's *Poetical Rhapsody* with the heading "This Hymn was sung by Amphitrite, Thamesis, and other Sea-Nymphs, in Gray's Inn Masque, at the Court, 1594." See my edition of the *Rhapsody.*

Page 202. "It was the frog in the well."—There are several versions of this delightful old ditty; the following is from Kirkpatrick Sharpe's *Ballad Book,* 1824 :—

> "There lived a puddy in a well,
> And a merry mouse in a mill.
>
> Puddy he'd a wooin ride,
> Sword and pistol by his side.
>
> Puddy came to the mouse's wonne,
> ' Mistress mouse, are you within ?'
>
> 'Yes, kind Sir, I am within ;
> Saftly do I sit and spin.'
>
> ' Madam. I am come to woo ;
> Marriage I must have of you.
>
> ' Marriage I will grant you nane,
> Until Uncle Rotten he comes hame.'
>
> ' Uncle Rotten's now come hame ;
> Fy ! gar busk the bride alang.'
>
> Lord Rotten sat at the head o' the table,
> Because he was baith stout and able.
>
> What is't that sit next the wa',
> But Lady Mouse, baith jimp and sma' ?

What is't that sits next the bride,
But the sola puddy, wi' his yellow side ?

Syne came the deuk, but and the drake ;
The deuk took puddy, and garred him squaik.

Then cam in the carl cat,
Wi' a fiddle on his back,
' Want ye ony music here ? '

The puddy he swam doun the brook ;
The drake he catched him in his fluke.

The cat he pu'd Lord Rotten doun ;
The kittens they did claw his croun.

But Lady Mouse, baith jimp and sma',
Crept into a hole beneath the wa' :
' Squeak ! ' quoth she, ' I'm weel awa'.' "

Doubtless Ravenscroft's version is more ancient. A
ballad entitled "A most strange weddinge of the frogge
and the mouse" was licensed for printing in 1580.

Page 204. " By the moon we sport and play . . .
And about, about go we."—From the anonymous play
(ascribed without evidence to Lyly), *The Maid's
Metamorphosis,* 1600.

Page 208. " And fortune's fate not fearing/ Sing
sweet in summer morning."—There is some corruption
here. Oliphant (*Musa Madrigalesca*) boldly reads
"And fickle fortune scorning."

Page 210. " Shall be play barley-break ? "—*Barley-
break* was an old rustic game, played by three couples.
It is elaborately described in the first book of Sidney's
Arcadia.

Page 212. " Little lawn then served the Pawn."—
The Pawn was a corridor, serving as a bazaar, in the
Royal Exchange (Gresham's).

LIST OF SONG-BOOKS.

MUNDY, JOHN. *Songs and Psalms,* 1594. 153, 194.
Musica Transalpina, The Second Book of Madrigals,
1597. 71, 170.

PEERSON, MARTIN. *Private Music,* 1620. 58, 61,
66, 89, 207.
PILKINGTON, FRANCIS. *The First Set of Madrigals
and Pastorals,* 1613. 81, 88, 124.
The Second Set of Madrigals, 1624. 95.
PORTER, WALTER. *Madrigals and Airs,* 1632. 172.

RAVENSCROFT, THOMAS. *Melismata,* 1611. 29, 202,
203.
*Brief Discourse of the true use of Charact'ring
the Degrees,* 1614. 204, 205, 206.
ROSSETER, PHILIP. *See* CAMPION, THOMAS.

VAUTOR, THOMAS. *Songs of divers Airs and
Natures,* 1619. 48, 195.

WEELKES, THOMAS. *Ballets and Madrigals,* 1598.
30, 117, 128.
Madrigals, 1597, 1600. 47, 84, 88, 97, 134, 147,
210.
Airs or Fantastic Spirits, 1608. 110, 209.
WILBYE, JOHN. *The First Set of English Madrigals,*
1598. 5, 33, 64, 71, 87, 117, 168.
The Second Set of English Madrigals, 1609. 26,
38, 49, 81, 129, 155, 183, 192.
WILSON, DR. JOHN. *Cheerful Airs or Ballads,* 1660.
130, 156.

Yonge, Nicholas.   See *Musica Transalpina.*

Add. MS. 18,936.   100.
Christ Church MS. I. 4. 78.   176.
  I. 5. 49.   5, 64, 111, 195, 204.
  K. 3. 43-5.   93, 187.

CHISWICK PRESS :—C. WHITTINGHAM AND CO., TOOKS COURT,
CHANCERY LANE.

www.ingramcontent.com/pod-product-compliance
Lightning Source LLC
Chambersburg PA
CBHW030352270326
41926CB00009B/1073